Romanoff

Prince of Rogues

Romanoff
Prince of Rogues

The Life & Times of a
Hollywood Icon

JANE PEJSA

Library of Congress Catalog Card Number 97-93326
International Standard Book Number 0-9612776-8-8

Edited and Composed by Barbara Field
Designed by Susan Bishop
Printed by Burgess Printing Company

Kenwood Publishing
1314 Marquette Avenue, Suite 906
Minneapolis, MN 55403-4105
Phone/Fax: 612-332-5073/5204
Web site: kenwoodpublishing.com

Cataloging-in-Publication Data
Pejsa, Jane, 1929–
    Romanoff—Prince of Rogues: The Life & Times of a
Hollywood Icon.
    Includes bibliography, index.
    1. Romanoff, Michael, 1890–1971. 2. Hollywood. 3.
Lithuania. 4. Rat Pack. 5. Restaurants, Romanoffs.

For my friend
Margot Auerbacher Siegel,
who urged me to write the tale

Contents

CONTENTS

With Friends Who Mattered

Illustrations

ILLUSTRATIONS

Preface

Earlier in this twentieth century—a more innocent time, they say—a blithe spirit streaked across the American scene. He was first noted in 1922, having arrived in New York by ship, later detained at Ellis Island for lack of identification, then escaping from the island by swimming ashore with his walking stick clenched between his teeth. In the golden years following victory in the First World War, he was celebrated from New York to California—Prince Michael Dimitri Alexandrovich Obolenski-Romanoff, nephew of the last Russian czar,* at times even the man who killed the wicked Rasputin.

Never mind that most every celebration of the prince was followed by an unmasking of his borrowed identity. He invariably brought good humor and diversion into some of the richest and most renowned circles of America. And if the Russian prince wore out his welcome, there were many others to take his place—the English gentleman Willoughby de Burke, artist Rockwell Kent, Professor John William Adams from Yale, Mr. R. A. Adams of New York, and a dozen more.

Through the Great Depression and into the Second World War, this bright spirit entertained and enlivened a

---

Tsar is the more accurate transliteration from Russian and in 1997 is considered the more acceptable written form. However, *czar* was the acceptable Americanized written form of the title in the time of Michael Romanoff and thus is used throughout this book.

society that was inclined not to look behind the mask. Better not to look, for blithe spirit had once been a difficult child in Vilna, Lithuania, sent unwillingly to America by his desperate mother. Camping out on the streets of New York and on other streets across the land, he had learned to survive in subways, under churchyard monuments, and behind the doorways of city buildings. This boy was Hershel Geguzin, for whom America was a land of overwhelming emptiness.

Recorded here is the incredible life journey of this seemingly lost immigrant child from loneliness and poverty to recognition as one of the most interesting and successful personalities in America—Prince Michael Romanoff, proprietor of Romanoffs in Beverly Hills, friend and restaurateur to Hollywood's greatest stars.

Early on, Prince Michael became the darling of the national press—*The New Yorker, The New York Times*, the *Los Angeles Times, The Saturday Evening Post, Life, Holiday*, and *Time*. Over and over, journalists recounted with amusement the escapades of this imposter prince. Mike Romanoff's adventures became a running gag that lasted more than a half century!

But the truth was not always so amusing. As researcher and author, I have endeavored to uncover the reality of Mike Romanoff's life journey as well as the key to his heart. In the first instance, I have had great success, uncovering material that no police department or immigration agency was able to come by and laying it all out as an unfolding drama. In the second instance, I have been less successful, for I still do not fully understand what lay in the prince's heart. There are a number of clues, however, and I have given each one high visibility in the course of writing this tale.

PREFACE

The life of Prince Michael Romanoff is a bittersweet romance—indeed a tragicomedy. It fascinates me no end. I believe the prince himself, with his own keen sense of the absurd, would likewise find this a captivating tale.

Minneapolis   JANE PEJSA
June 1997

Acknowledgments

Some three years ago, Professor Elizabeth Nissen invited me to tea in her home. It was an invitation with a broader purpose, for this long-time family friend wanted to talk to me about a man she once knew—an acquaintance from the fall of 1922 when she was studying at the Sorbonne in Paris. With clearly mixed emotions, Professor Nissen recalled her encounter with the man who would later be known as Prince Michael Romanoff. Her vivid description of the would-be prince so piqued my curiosity that I could not let him go, even though at the time I was working on another research project. That project necessitated frequent visits to both the public library and the university library. Thus I acquired the habit of looking up information on this Romanoff imposter every time I visited either institution.

Over many such visits, I found that much of his adult life had been chronicled by major periodicals. Yes, one could write a book just using these materials, but it would require much more if ever I should choose to record the life journey of such an intriguing character.

Thus I determined to dig deeper by seeking out those who might have known the unlikely prince. My first fortunate encounter was with Kurt Niklas, proprietor of Bistro Gardens, a charming Los Angeles eatery. Over lunch, Kurt spoke to me about his years with Mike Romanoff. For more than a decade, Kurt Niklas had been on the staff of

xv

Romanoffs. His memories shed significant light not only on Mike Romanoff in his later years but also on Hollywood film society at a time when Romanoffs was undisputably the restaurant of the stars.

Some months later, I was privileged to meet Mike Romanoff's nephew, Dr. Emmanuel Piore of New York. He and Mrs. Piore consented to be interviewed and in this way I first learned about Mike Romanoff's family roots and especially his sister Olga, Dr. Piore's mother, with whom Mike maintained a lifelong bond. Through the Piores I was introduced to Mike Romanoff's grandniece Dahlia Friedman, also of New York. Later, through Dahlia, I met her mother, Mike's niece—Nina Marshak Papermacher of Haifa, Israel. Over Sunday brunch in New York, with Dahlia faithfully interpreting between the Polish and English languages, Nina spoke of her family's noble history, its tragic fate during the Holocaust, and her dramatic meeting with this fabled American uncle after the war.

Later I was able to flesh out Mike Romanoff's American childhood from material gleaned in a remarkable conversation with Robert Bliss of Hillsboro, Illinois. He shared with me not only his own observations of the prince during two feted visits to Hillsboro, in 1923 and 1936, but also those of his father, for Clint Bliss had once attended school with the mysterious New York orphan.

In addition to those who shared firsthand memories of Michael Romanoff, a number of others also made significant contributions to this chronicle: Idabel Evans and David Jackson each spent hours gathering details of the prince's Illinois childhood from uncataloged newspaper archives; Gloria Hogan brought to light a number of Prince Michael vignettes; Sue Zelickson ferreted out the origins of "Strawberries Romanoff"; Dana Broccoli, Roger Childers, Hal Kanter, Fred Sill, Gretchen Van der Weide, and Richard Zanuck all were helpful one way or another in leading me to Kurt Niklas and Gloria Romanoff. David Brown, Hume

ACKNOWLEDGMENTS

Cronyn, Alistair Cooke, and Mia Farrow graciously granted me permission to quote from their own published works.

Dr. Jonathan Jensen, Professor of Psychiatry at the University of Minnesota, read the completed tale sympathetically yet critically. He has added his own remarks, thus providing a deeper insight into the curious life journey of this extraordinary man.

My sincere thanks to all those named here, to others named in the Bibliography, to Barbara Field, whose skillful editing clarified the prose without compromising either the style or the content of the tale, and to Susan Bishop, whose book design gave life to the outcome.

Finally and foremost, I thank my husband, Arthur. His support has been constant throughout this entire adventure, his chapter-by-chapter critiques have all been well taken, and I believe his expectations have been fulfilled.

In Search of Identity

April 1932

Nowhere on the Seven Seas was there a passenger ship to compare with the French flagship *Ile de France*. Launched five years earlier when Europe was experiencing a short-lived frenzy of prosperity, this queen of the seas was nothing less than magnificent. Almost eight hundred feet in length, her most acclaimed feature was a central interior foyer that towered three decks in height. Surrounding this massive space were two levels of balconies and a pair of grand staircases on which first-class passengers could descend like royalty from their luxurious cabins to the foyer below. In fact, throughout the ship, the interiors ensured France's leadership in matters of style—the newest and the latest in art deco design. From the moment of her launching, the *Ile de France* was the ship against which all subsequent passenger liners were measured. For years after, first-class passage on this flagship of the French fleet would be the preferred transit for the "best" people from many nations.

By 1932, however, prosperity had given way to economic decline, not only in France but in neighboring nations as well. This was the year that a worldwide depression seemed to have settled in for keeps. Thus the spring crossing of the *Ile de France* from Le Havre to New York, always an occasion for celebration, found the first-class deck far from full. Still the passenger list had never glittered more brilliantly, and those aboard could congratulate themselves on the quality of their traveling companions, which more than compensated for any empty first-class cabins. Begin with The Maestro. Arturo Toscanini, the world's premier orchestra conductor, was making the trip to conduct a single concert at Carnegie Hall, this for the benefit of unemployed New York musicians. Besides the maestro and his accompanist, there was Michael Clemenceau, son of the late Georges Clemenceau, that great French premier who led France to victory in the World War and who afterward dictated the new map of Europe. Just to meet the son of such a man was reason enough to book first class if one could afford it in the year 1932. In addition to these luminaries, a number of memorable but lesser lights were on board, including the former governor-general of the Belgian Congo, the president of the French War Veterans Association, and an American woman from Cleveland who had made three trips on Germany's new lighter-than-air transport—the *Graf Zeppelin.*

* * *

First night at sea, the captain's ball, and a crowd gathered in the grand foyer before late dinner. Handkerchiefs are waved, greetings exchanged, and even kisses blown between those looking down over the balcony railings and those looking up from below. Soon the balconies empty out as, one by one, or more often in pairs, the remaining guests descend to the foyer. The scene is absolutely unmatched in elegance.

But look—sweeping down the left staircase are two well-turned-out dowagers, each on one arm of a much younger man whose imperial bearing almost masks his very short stature. His dress alone merits attention—full tuxedo, obviously tailor-made, shirt cuffs emblazoned with an imperial monogram of gold thread, and a gold-tipped walking stick held between his hands. Eyes turn. One of the women whispers to an acquaintance—"Grand Duke Michael Romanoff, brother of the late czar." The listener takes note. This must be the pretender to the throne, recalling that not only the czar but his wife and five children were all murdered by the Bolsheviks. In deference to the grand duke, the crowd steps back that the trio might make its way to an empty table. One of the dowagers orders champagne after asking His Highness to select his preferred label. Now others crowd in while the Russian engages his companions in a dignified repartee that only enhances his majestic qualities. His command of the language is impressive, pure Oxonian with only a touch of the Continent. Clearly the grand duke was raised with an English governess. These are magical moments, and they portend a voyage of great adventure. Such is the mood in the grand foyer of the *Ile de France*.

Later, on entering the dining salon, the Russian bids adieu to each of his ladies, with a deep bow and a kiss on the hand. This evening he will dine with Edward Cudahy, Jr., of New York, who has connections to his New York Romanoff relatives. They have matters to discuss, especially the imperial jewels held in London, which will probably be released to the family before the year is out. And so Edward Cudahy and his fortunate table companions take pleasure in the company of Michael Dimitri Alexandrovich Romanoff. But the grand duke? Didn't the Bolsheviks admit to having executed him? Of course, of course, agrees Romanoff. The gentleman must have misunderstood earlier. He, Michael Alexandrovich Romanoff, is the son of the czar's brother, and he eschews the title of grand duke. "Prince Michael" is sufficient, and in any case, when it comes to the company of Americans, he would much rather be just plain *Mister* Romanoff.

So it goes as the days and nights add up on this pleasure-filled springtime voyage. Mornings the prince can be found

in the lounge, discussing affairs of the day with other gentlemen, enjoying a pipeful of tobacco. Edward Cudahy
makes it a point to join the grand duke here, for he finds
the Russian to be a delightful raconteur. Afternoons the
prince promenades on deck in a smartly cut golf suit,
politely giving his attention to the ladies who lie in wait
along the way.

But it is the nights that truly belong to this "Prince of all
the Russias," and they always begin with his grand descent to
the foyer at a respectable time before the late dining hour.
He is invariably besieged by a growing circle of admirers
who want to know about his Romanoff past. Yes, he still suf-
fers nightmares for his part in the death of the wicked monk
Grigory Rasputin. The fall of the imperial government
came so soon after that murderous night that subsequent
events masked the horror of the deed. Only now, during the
quiet days of this sea voyage, have the implications of it all
begun to surface on the prince's psyche. It is not really
something he is proud of, for he has always been averse to
violence. It simply had to be done in order to save Mother
Russia. The tragedy is that he acted too late.

How did it come about? Oh, it was a marvelous deception, in which the czarina played an unwitting part. The czar
was in the field commanding the Russian armies, leaving
the czarina to govern the nation at war. Always the evil
monk was present, filling her head with the kind of non-
sense that drove the population into the hands of the revo-
lutionaries. Prince Michael alone could reason with her,
and he alone could convince her that an evening's entertainment for Rasputin in St. Petersburg might benefit them
all. And so Grigory joined the prince in a carriage provided
by the czarina herself. They were to visit the palace of a
mutual companion, and such debauchery did the prince
promise Rasputin, for that is the kind of man the monk was.
After reaching the palace of the accomplice, the prince and
the host escorted Rasputin to the billiard room, where the

monk accepted the offer of a drink. It was poison-laced to bring him down; yet the evil man appeared to be unfazed. Then Prince Michael's companion pulled his pistol and fired. The monk collapsed, but he was only wounded. As he rose to leap at his assailant, Prince Michael was forced to fire his own pistol. Rasputin fell, never to rise again. They carried his body to a bridge and threw it into the Neva River.

Prince Michael's voice breaks. He reaches for his linen handkerchief and gently dabs an eye. If only he could leave behind these wretched memories, along with the even more wretched ones of all that happened to him later. His rapt listeners understand. A glass of champagne is ordered for His Highness—this voyage should be a time of joy, not tears.

It is time for dinner now—the final call. Prince Michael makes his way to the dining salon, chatting amiably with the lady or gentleman whose guest he will be for the evening. It turns out there are not enough nights at sea to accommodate all the invitations extended to the prince during the voyage.

Yet amidst all the grandeur, there are curious inconsistencies, none of them very serious. When a passenger tries to engage the grand duke in a Russian conversation, he politely waves the man aside. "No, no, no. We shall not speak Russian; I must learn your English." When another passenger looks up the prince's cabin number, hoping to deliver an invitation for cocktails, it is found to be unlisted. Out of respect for his privacy, no doubt. A steward also is puzzled when a stranger asks him to replace his lost cabin key. But it still might all have worked out comfortably were it not for an unfortunate occurrence the last night at sea.

Edward Cudahy is seated for dinner at the captain's table. The two men reminisce about the previous days of the voyage, finding themselves in total agreement. Such a splendid group of passengers—the elegantly attired ladies, gentlemen of the highest quality, and scintillating conversation throughout. Cudahy remarks that Prince Michael

7

Romanoff, especially, illuminated the evenings of so many passengers, for he was a most entertaining raconteur. "The prince?" inquires the captain. Cudahy qualifies his assertion by referring to "Grand Duke Michael," a title the prince nowadays eschews. The captain is alarmed. "There are no grand dukes on board this ship, nor any Romanoffs that I know of!"

* * *

Prince Michael was arrested that night, still dressed in his stiff shirt and tuxedo. Before placing him in the ship's brig, officers tore off his elegantly monogrammed shirt cuffs— half sheets of the ship's stationery embossed with the *Ile de France's* gold crest.

1

Hershel Geguzin

Most investigators believe [Hershel] was born about 1890 in Brooklyn, New York. However, Cincinnati, Ohio, Hillsboro, Illinois, and Tyler, Texas, are runners-up. The Immigration Service held that he was born overseas, but moved to New York at age three.[1]

The Geguzin name is as old as the oldest Jewish community in Lithuania, older even than the historic Ghetto at Vilna.* The village whence came the name once lay thirty kilometers southwest of Vilna,* in the District of Trokai. It had existed at least since the fifteenth century, when the great Polish–Lithuanian empire reached from the Baltic to the Black Sea. When Jews were hounded out of lands in western Europe, they could always take sanctuary in this sprawling kingdom. And so they did, for at least three hundred years, until they comprised ten percent of the population in ethnic Lithuania. A fervent religious spirit reigned among these people, spawning a renaissance in philosophy and literature that would have been prohibited in western Europe. And one great center of all this was indeed the city of Vilna.

But times change, and likewise the balance of power. By the late eighteenth century, the once invincible Polish–

---

*Under Russian rule: *Vilna;* as part of Poland, 1922–1941: *Wilno;* Lithuanian since 1944: *Vilniaus.*

9

Lithuanian empire had been eclipsed on three sides by a triumvirate of competing powers, each coveting a part of the fading Slavic empire. Three times within a quarter century the empire was partitioned until every piece of these ancient lands was controlled either by Prussia, Russia, or Austria–Hungary. Ethnic Lithuania, including the city of Vilna, fell to Imperial Russia; it was incorporated into the empire as simply the "Territory of the Northwest."

And this was but the beginning. Over successive decades, a policy of russianization was implemented with such severe measures as to profoundly alter the lives of all who inhabited the land—the ancient Balts and the Poles as well as the Jews. Each ethnic group responded in its own way as increasingly restrictive proscriptions were applied to language, education, and religion. The Jewish response was generally one of consolidation. Jewish villages in the countryside disappeared as entire families and clans migrated into the cities for mutual support and protection. It was on this account that the clan called Geguzin, having dwelt in the Lithuanian kingdom for half a millennium, found its way from the Geguzin village into the city of Vilna.

In 1889, where this tale begins, more than forty percent of Vilna's inhabitants were Jews. Most lived in the ghetto, a place of bustling energy—economic as well as intellectual. These Jews were tradesmen and craftsmen—millers, bakers, tailors, harness-makers, plasterers, glaziers, blacksmiths, wagon drivers, and porters. Although not many became rich, few were poverty-stricken either. This was a community of plain, hardworking, sober, and modest people, and it might have continued indefinitely but for the capricious rule of czarist Russia.

Oddly enough, the family to which our attention is drawn here—the family of Hinde and Emmanuel Geguzin—did not live in the ghetto, though their livelihood was based there. In the year 1889, they and their five small children occupied a flat at Traku 11, in Vilna's "new town," while their family dry goods establishment served a market that encompassed virtually the entire city. In comparison to their neighbors and kinsmen, the Geguzins of Vilna were well-to-do and cosmopolitan. At home as wife and mother, Hinde Geguzin ruled a household where only Yiddish was spoken. As partner in business with Emmanuel, she was also conversant in Russian, in Polish, and in Lithuanian. Such were the requirements of successful tradesmen in Russian Lithuania.

Of all the discomforts in life that derived from Russian rule—restricted opportunities and stultifying regulations—more fearsome by far was the chronic expectation of a pogrom. It might not come for years, and it might descend upon the Jews at any moment. One had no way of knowing when and where a regiment of Russian soldiers, perhaps aided by groups of civilians, would swoop down into the ghetto, crash through the streets and into the homes—sometimes to slay indiscriminately the young and the old, and more often to carry off the most promising of the young men, who would never be seen again.

Granted these uncertainties, the Geguzins of Vilna nonetheless lived a peaceful existence—until the autumn of 1889. Emmanuel Geguzin had traveled to Warsaw on business. Strolling along the principal avenue, he came upon two men engaged in a violent struggle, one having been thrown to the ground. A peacemaker by nature, Emmanuel went to rescue the victim. The assailant struck him so violently that he too fell to the ground, never to rise again.

The following February, Hinde Geguzin, now widowed and the mother of five children, gave birth to her sixth child, a son, whom she named Hershel.

Hardly granted time to mother her infant son, let alone time to mourn her husband, Hinde Geguzin took over the family business. So suited was she to the task that in subsequent years her wares included not only bolts of cloth but most any item that a tailor or seamstress might require. In addition, she expanded the business by establishing her own tailoring enterprise and thus became the sole supplier of uniforms for the Vilna police force. Nor was that all. In the first years of the twentieth century, Hinde Geguzin acquired the exclusive Singer Sewing Machine franchise for Russia's entire "Territory of the Northwest."

In her own mind, this mother was building a family enterprise, a business that in time would be taken over by one of her several sons or daughters. Each in turn was given the appropriate education for the task. From age six, he or she studied religion at the Heder, along with arithmetic, geography, and reading and writing in the Yiddish language.

It was expected that all of the children would work in the tailoring shop when not in school. Each one began with the hand sewing—buttons and buttonholes—then moved on to machine sewing and steam pressers, and finally to the cutting. Thus each child learned every task in the business. The mother's expectation was, of course, that by the time the sons completed the Heder and made their bar mitzvahs, they would be somewhat accomplished tailors. But that was not enough. Both sons and daughters must also be educated in the Russian high school system, for without the "Russian" education, their careers and lives would forever be constrained. Such was the plan of this Jewish mother as she raised her family alone, always under the constant surveillance of the Russian authorities.

By the turn of the century, Hinde's efforts were bearing fruit, though not entirely as she had expected. Across the Russian empire, among nationalities of every kind, political unrest was building. The young Czar Nicholas had recently ascended the throne, and those who had expected the best from him were quickly disappointed. Hinde's first-born son, Pina, had completed his education but, instead of taking over the family enterprise, had gone off to Moscow to seek his fortune and, as the mother feared, to participate in the

Ghetto Street in Vilna, watercolor by Lionel Reiss
From *My Subjects Were Jews*, New York: Gordon Press, 1938

still undefined revolution that was to come. Not long after, her second son, Yuri, followed his brother to Moscow.

Olga, the oldest daughter, was close to completing her high school education. She ran the household as well. Thus onto her fell the major responsibility of raising young Hershel, the child who had never known his father. The boy, now nine, attended the Heder, but his education was not going smoothly. Certainly the boy did not lack wit. He was bright and quick, and when it suited him, captivating as well. But Hershel was undependable, especially when it came to completing the tailoring tasks his mother assigned to him. And when it came to school, he was positively defiant. He would absent himself frequently and, when confronted by his mother or older siblings, would disappear from home for days.

Clearly the son's behavior had gotten beyond the mother's control. Not only was Hershel's future education, hence livelihood, in jeopardy, but his life as well. An errant boy such as he, out beyond the protective cocoon of the Jewish community, was subject to kidnapping and worse. It would not require a pogrom for the runaway boy to be captured, perhaps tortured or otherwise assaulted and possibly slain, by a band of drunken soldiers. Under such premises as these the mother was forced to act.

Hinde Geguzin consulted with trusted men in the community. It was agreed that Hershel should be sent away, out of danger, to a land where the law protected its citizens, a place where Hershel's exuberance might flower and his waywardness be tamed. That land was America, and the place was New York. In the decade of the nineties, thousands of Jews had emigrated from Lithuania to America. The opportunity presented itself when Hinde's cousin Joseph Bloomberg announced that he was leaving with his family for New York. Joseph consented to add Hershel's name to the family passport so as to slip him past both the Russian and American authorities as one of his own. Hinde found the arrangement acceptable and handed over to her cousin a bag of gold rubles. The mother could be generous. It was only the son who had not been consulted.

Thus, in the spring of 1900, when Hershel Geguzin was just ten years old, his mother dressed him in a new short worsted wool coat with long trousers, tailored for him from the same material as the Vilna police uniforms. She packed a little carpetbag for him, including a few tools of the tailoring trade. If it didn't work out with the Bloombergs, he could always make his way as a tailoring apprentice. Unbeknown to Hershel, she had also sewn into his pockets a few gold rubles.

It was left to Olga, however, to deliver the boy and his carpetbag to the railroad station. In the few short years of Hershel's childhood, it was she who had mothered him most. Brother and sister wept mightily at the parting. Each knew that those who went to America would never see Vilna again. Nor was Olga to follow later, for her lot lay with the family and the business. It was a wrenching parting indeed when the boy finally let go of his sister's hand and reluctantly followed along behind his uncle's children, for whom he had little affection.

By train to the ancient Hanseatic port of Danzig, then by ferry to Bremen, that hub of transatlantic travel, and finally on a steamer of the North German Lloyd—Hershel Geguzin was on his way to America.

2

Harry Gaygussen/ Gerguson/Ferguson

I was born in New York, where my father died when I was six years old. I do not remember my mother. After my father's death, I was taken in charge by a society that cared for homeless children and I was sent to a family living on a farm near Edwardsville [Illinois]. They agreed to let me work for my board and clothes and send me to school, but they didn't send me to school and I ran away several times.

Finally, the woman representing the orphan society came for me, and we were on the train, and she was giving me a lecture on how I should behave, when a gentleman sitting in the seat behind us overheard her conversation, and he arose, introduced himself as Col. Kronk, and stated that he was operating a farm near Hillsboro and he offered to take me in, give me a home and an education. He promised me $15 per month and my board and clothes, and after working for him for three months, during which time he starved me, paid me nothing and mistreated me, I ran away.[1]

The New York City that greeted young Hershel Geguzin was hardly yet a melting pot. Rather it resembled a boiling cauldron when it came to population, economics, and the city landscape itself. The city was pressed to accommodate an urban population growing by more than 100,000 each year. New York's Jewish population alone would increase from 80,000 to a million within just three decades.

17

Unlike earlier Jewish immigrants, who generally hailed from German-speaking lands, these new immigrants came primarily out of eastern Europe, and especially out of the lands ruled by the Russian czar, of which Lithuania was but one. Their common language was Yiddish; in religion they were orthodox, in politics socialist, and above all they were poor.

The Lower East Side was to become the place these Jews called home. By the time Hershel and the Bloombergs arrived, these newcomers had virtually replaced a previous generation of Irish immigrants who were moving uptown on Manhattan as well as up from poverty. The place where Hershel's family found shelter was in the heart of this Lower East Side, at 28 Monroe Street. It was an upstairs flat in a four-story tenement, perched on a twenty-foot lot. The family probably shared a single water source with other residents of the building, and there surely were no indoor plumbing facilities. At this late date we know little more, only that young Hershel, on his arrival, was thoroughly dismayed: How could his mother have thrust her own son into such abysmal conditions?

The neighborhood itself spoke to the rapidity of change. In the block behind the Bloomberg flat stood a synagogue, a public elementary school, and a Catholic church with its own school attached. Across the street were a soap factory, a barrel factory, and a cooper's shop, and in between, as far as the eye could see, row upon row of brownstone tenement dwellings teeming with immigrant families much like the Bloombergs.

Hershel did not like his new family at all, nor did he like the environment. He didn't understand the language at school, and he had no interest in visiting the synagogue. This may have been the New World where nothing resembled the old, but the boy was still Hershel Geguzin, his mother's most difficult child—the boy who ran away rather than be forced to go to school.

At home in Vilna, Hershel had already made brief forays into independence—disappearing from home, sleeping in an empty shed, begging food from a street vendor, and sweeping floors to earn food from shopkeepers. By the time he was ten years old, he had more than mastered the art of surviving on his own, all the while observing and learning from the world about him. In Vilna, the mother acted as best she could to thwart these escapades, but she never allowed word of her problems to reach the authorities. She trusted them not at all.

In New York, the uncle could well throw up his hands in despair over the ungrateful and incorrigible child with which he had been saddled. He could notify the school and even gain sympathy from the truant officer who came to fetch the absent boy. Bloomberg could share his frustration. He had tried beating the boy, locking him up, even denying him his dinner, all to no avail. The boy had simply disappeared, and for Bloomberg at least, it was good riddance. It was under these adverse conditions that the transformation of Hershel Geguzin commenced.

In the wee hours of a winter morning, a night watchman found the boy asleep on the pool table of an East Side Democratic club. He recognized him as the newspaper boy from the corner at East Broadway. The child's overcoat was in rags and his clothes not much better. Not so unusual in this first decade of the twentieth century, when the street children of New York, whether orphaned, abandoned, or simply delinquent, had become the scandal of a nation. Since, in this thoroughly American city, there was a solution for every problem, New York boasted children's institutions of every stripe, ready to serve every needy segment of the population.

For such a case as this, the New York Society for the Prevention of Cruelty to Children was called to take charge. They interviewed the boy and determined that he was about

Orchard Street on New York's Lower East Side, watercolor by Lionel Reiss
From *My Subjects Were Jews,* New York: Gordon Press, 1938

twelve years old and had come to this country with his parents two years earlier, that he was Jewish, and that both his parents had died without making application for U.S. citizenship. For such a child the institution of choice was the Manhattan Hebrew orphanage. Hershel was taken there and duly registered as Harry Gaygussen, an orphan whose guardian was unable to care for him. It was a short stay, however, for the boy was wont to run away and otherwise confound his caregivers. Before too long the Hebrew orphanage labeled him incorrigible. Harry was turned over to the New York Juvenile Asylum, an institution that accepted children referred by the court system. They were generally children who had come to the attention of the police, either through their own misadventures or because of serious neglect at home.

The Juvenile Asylum owned an institution at Dobbs Ferry—the Children's Village—which occupied 277 beautiful acres north of the city on the Hudson River. The campus was laid out with homelike cottages arranged in neighborhood clusters. The children's medical needs, their education, their recreation activities, and even religious instruction were all taken care of within the confines of the village. The children were not meant to stay at the village indefinitely, for the driving philosophy of the institution was that of "placing out." A better term might have been "indentured service," for from the earliest days of the asylum, both boys and girls were routinely signed over to rural households to be held in bondage until they reached maturity.

Harry Gaygussen probably first entered the Children's Village in 1903, when placing out was accepted as the best way to instill moral values, education, and industrious habits in the children who came under its care. He was reined in, so to speak, finally compelled to attend school, and indeed he profited immensely from it. By 1905, the boy could not only speak like a true New York adolescent, he could also read and write the English language fluently.

Here at the Children's Village, "Gaygussen" became "Gerguson," probably at the behest of a social worker whose aim above all was to place out "americanized" children. Years later Harry would vehemently deny the name "Gerguson," saying he had never even been consulted in the matter.

Education at the Village also meant learning how to treat adults, especially those in the higher classes—how to respond to them and how to please them—for the ultimate goal of the Children's Village was to arrange situations whereby their wards would not be returned. These lessons may well have been the most important skills Harry learned at the Children's Village, for indeed they drove his life journey.

When it came time for placing out, the Children's Aid Society took over. A Village child would be outfitted with a new set of clothes and sent west out of New York by train in the company of other children and a temporary guardian. At towns along the way, they would disembark and be paraded before the interested populace. A contract of sorts would be arranged whereby each child was bound over to an adult—the child to work for his board, room, and clothing, the adult to promise a good environment, schooling, and modest spending money until the child's maturity— eighteen years for girls and twenty-one years for boys. With goodwill on both sides, it was a system that could work very well.

Illinois was a favorite destination for the Children's Village when it came to placing out. First of all, the state of Illinois permitted indentured service. In addition, by the late nineteenth century, three major railroads crisscrossed the state. Thus, at age fifteen, Harry Gerguson traveled from Dobbs Ferry, New York, to Hillsboro, Illinois, by rail, under the auspices of the Children's Aid Society. There he was bound over to an Edwardsville farmer, whose name has been lost in history. If one can believe Harry's memory, the experiment was a disaster. The most lasting impact appears to have been in the new family name that Harry selected for himself—Ferguson. He borrowed it from a neighboring farmer, Charles Ferguson. Thus was born Harry Ferguson.

The details of Harry Ferguson's journey from Edwardsville to Hillsboro are somewhat sketchy but not that important. He apparently came under the care of one Judge Kronk. Kronk was said to be a St. Louis lawyer who owned a farm near Hillsboro. Records indicate that Harry may have attended a rural school while in Kronk's employ. How long he remained on the farm is not clear, but the residents of Hillsboro first discovered the boy in the summer of 1906. He was sleeping in the yard of the Presbyterian Church. If the weather was inclement, he retreated to the hallway entrance of a business building on Main Street. The townspeople became fascinated with the young stranger. The town policeman took pity and invited the boy to sleep in his office. Shopkeepers engaged Harry to run their errands that he might always have money for food, and the tailor engaged him to operate the steam presser—finding him to be the cleverest ever when it came to pressing pants. So recalled a Hillsboro resident. Later the town memories were more picturesque:

> Young Ferguson was a rather attractive looking boy, with coal black hair, dark complexion and black, piercing eyes, and he had a most wonderful imagination. He resembled an Italian or a dark-skinned foreigner in appearance, and as nothing was known here regarding his parentage, those who knew him always believed he had assumed the name Ferguson in order to hide his real identity and nationality.[3]

Whatever the lad's origins, it was clear to the good folk of Hillsboro that he needed proper shelter. Frank McDavid, the local banker, came forward and offered Harry an attic room in his large home. McDavid enrolled the sixteen-year-old boy in the seventh grade of Winhold Elementary School. Saddled in a classroom where he was undoubtedly the oldest, Harry was nevertheless in luck. His teacher, one Miss Betty Coale, understood what drove this thoroughly undisciplined adolescent. She was strict with him, even using a paddle when the occasion demanded. But she gave him what he needed most—much attention along with high expectations. Under Miss Coale's tutelage, Harry absorbed all that she had to teach in language, in math, and especially in history and geography. His school attendance was exemplary—just three absences in the entire year. Likewise his report card was better than satisfactory, with 97 in spelling and 92 in rhetoricals. He was a passionate reader, devouring every geography book in the library. The townspeople discovered in Harry a fascinating adventurer and storyteller whose imagination had taken him to the far corners of the world. By the end of the year, Miss Coale declared Harry her star student, while Harry declared this teacher his first love.

The relationship between Harry and Frank McDavid was not so fortunate. Over the summer, McDavid found it necessary to chide the boy continually for not doing the work assigned to him. With Harry this had no effect. The more the banker scolded, the more estranged the boy became. Finally, McDavid ordered Harry to pack his clothes and leave. Harry retreated to his attic room, packed together his belongings, and railed out loud against this betrayal by his benefactor. McDavid was not deaf, and he too started up the stairway to the attic. On hearing footsteps, Harry began to pray. In a loud voice, he asked the Lord to make him a better boy and help him to behave. But it was too late for McDavid, who had also heard what came before.

Harry Ferguson bade an emotional farewell to his friends on Main Street. No mention of Mr. McDavid, rather a declaration that he was on his way to Washington, D.C. He had just been appointed a Congressional page, sure proof of his

Bellboy Harry Ferguson in the Litchfield Hotel, ca. 1907
Courtesy David Jackson, Litchfield, Illinois

successful americanization, all thanks to the good people of Hillsboro, and especially to Miss Coale.

The reality, however, did not quite live up to the dream. A few days after leaving Hillsboro, Harry turned up in the neighboring town of Litchfield. There he found a new benefactor and was enrolled in high school. Beginning in November, every day before school, Harry stoked four large furnaces in the town business buildings. After school he donned a smart little uniform and worked as a bellboy at the Litchfield Hotel.

But there were problems at school. The superintendent, C. E. Richmond, believed that high school students should behave in the classroom and take their studies seriously. In the previous school year, he had already expelled several students who did not live up to his standards. At that time, there had been an uproar on the school board, for several of these students were from the "best" families. Mr. Richmond, however, held his ground. Now in the fall of 1907, when Harry did not live up to Mr. Richmond's stringent demands, the superintendent had no qualms about suspending this outsider. Harry did not take the suspension lightly. The following day he went to Mr. Richmond's office to discuss the matter; Mr. Richmond not only pushed him out of the office, but with the help of the janitor, he threw him down an entire flight of stairs.

There was a huge outpouring of sympathy for the boy, both in Litchfield and in Hillsboro. In fact, Charles Bliss, owner of the *Hillsboro Journal,* published a passionate editorial on the subject: "For a Defenseless Boy." On a complaint by Harry Ferguson, the state charged the superintendent and janitor with assault and battery. Both pleaded innocent, and a court date was set.

In December, the case came to trial in a packed courtroom. Harry presented his version of events very well. Other students who had witnessed the event generally corroborated his testimony. Mr. Richmond, however, told a different story. Harry might have prevailed had not Mr. Richmond's attorney brought to the stand a number of Hillsboro residents who testified as to the boy's wild imagination and his less-than-truthful statements. After a three-day trial and two ballots, the jury returned a unanimous verdict: "Not guilty."

Harry Ferguson left Litchfield, vowing never to return.

3

A Rogue of Uncertain Origin

I came to St. Louis from Hillsboro with the hope of getting work and attending high school, but found it quite impossible. So I walked part of the way and rode in freight cars the other part to Tarrytown, New York, where I asked permission to attend a boys' private school and work for my tuition and lodging. I was informed that such an arrangement was most extraordinary and would not possibly be made, but the master, a kind man, told me of a school in New Hampshire where I might matriculate under such an arrangement.

I walked to that school, convinced the master that I was deserving and was admitted. I remained a year. I had read a great deal about Oxford University in England. I was determined to go to school there. I was then in my sixteenth year. That summer I ventured to sea on the steamship Philadelphia *as a scrub boy, working for my passage to Southampton.*

I left the ship at that port and, remaining there for a time, eventually reached London, where I found employment in an office after school hours. The first weekend I walked to Oxford to see the place. I found that everything of which I had dreamed was true and decided to remain there. I obtained work in a hotel where in the course of time I met one of the dons of Oxford. I told him of my secret ambition.

He explained that it was necessary to know Greek in order to matriculate and he offered to coach me in Greek and other studies. I accepted and when eighteen years old took the examinations and won a scholarship which carried with it a reward of 250 pounds.[4]

I remained there until I graduated, just before the outbreak of the war. When the war started, I enlisted at once and was sent to France with a dozen of my classmates. I think I am the only surviving man of this number. Two of these young men were sons of a wealthy nobleman, and one of these was recognized as one of the brightest young men England has produced in years. He and his brother were both killed in action within a few weeks of each other. One of the young men was a very particular dear friend of mine and at his death he left me 500 pounds. I was rapidly advanced in rank and participated in the battle of the Marne [France], where I was wounded. I was sent back into service and was again wounded, and was then sent to Gallipoli [Italy], where I was wounded on board before we disembarked. I was wounded four times while in service and incapacitated once by climatic conditions, but I remained in the service and at the close of the war I held the commission of Major, with a salary of 1,000 pounds a year.[5]

It is not certain whether Harry returned to the Children's Village after his Illinois adventure. Reports indicate that one more outplacement was attempted, that Harry was sent to a ranch near Bullard, Texas, and that the experiment did not succeed. Clearly the educational goals of Harry Ferguson were not compatible with the philosophy of the Dobbs Ferry Children's Village.

In 1909, at age nineteen, Harry signed onto a cattle ship and worked his way from New York to Southampton in England. So began his love affair with the language and culture of the British upper classes. In the decade that followed, a most remarkable metamorphosis took place whereby the street boy of New York evolved into an English gentleman. Details of the transformation were never really documented, but the outline is clear. Harry Ferguson's talent for mimicking was second only to his capacity for acquiring knowledge and adapting to circumstances.

For a time, he resided at Oxford, applying the skills he had learned as a child in Vilna. For certain he worked as a presser and mender in a clothing repair shop. He may also have been a private valet to one or more Oxford students, for this was a customary role in those days. Harry's precise circumstances become of little importance here. What is extraordinary is the fact that he acquired not only the accent and manners of the British aristocracy, but also an incredible store of anecdotal information regarding Eton, Cambridge, and Oxford. So familiar was he with all three institutions that he could gossip knowingly about the drinking establishments frequented by the students and hint at confidentialities when it came to the peccadilloes of certain faculty members.

Yet for all of his innate talent and acquired knowledge, Harry possessed a naïveté that would be his undoing. He assumed that in England, as he had observed in America, by acquiring the trappings of the upper classes—language, manners, interests, garb, and all that defined a "gentleman"—he would indeed be one of them. Not so. In England Harry Ferguson was nothing! To overcome this obstacle, the young man assumed a new persona, that of the aristocratic Willoughby de Burke. This led to the acquisition of new friends, and along with them entrée into London's best clubs. In this way did the young man come to the attention of the authorities. Scotland Yard mounted an investigation but had little success in identifying the imposter. In their files, Harry was simply labeled "a Rogue of Uncertain Origin."

Now it is no doubt true that, historically, the English justice system was far ahead of that in neighboring lands on the continent, at least when it came to the sort of crimes that often accompany serious social conditions. But tampering with the English aristocracy? Impersonating one of them? For this the British government, in 1915, placed Harry under a deportation order—an order that unfortunately could not be executed, for after 1914 most of Europe was at war. For the protection of British subjects, especially those of the aristocracy, the would-be Willoughby de Burke was incarcerated first in a mental institution and then in a Liverpool prison, to remain there for the duration of the conflict. Oddly enough, Harry's personal Waterloo occurred just at the time his family in Vilna was undergoing calamities far more devastating.

In June of 1914, a Serbian nationalist had assassinated Archduke Franz Ferdinand of the Austro–Hungarian Empire, nephew and designated successor to the aging Emperor Franz Joseph. It was a poor time to commit such a reckless act, for Europe was clearly divided into two armed camps, each side firmly secured through military alliances. In August the First World War erupted, pitting Austria–Hungary and Germany against the Triple Entente—Russia, France, and the British Empire. The Russian czar, already considerably weakened by internal pressures, found it necessary to bolster his military force through a mass conscription. And in czarist Russia, mass conscription traditionally meant invading the villages and towns throughout the land to conscript the eligible young men. Wherever the Russian czar ruled, it was conventional wisdom that the young men conscripted under these conditions were never to be seen again.

In the fall of 1914, a military conscription force swept through Russia's Northwest Territory and entered the city of Vilna. Hinde Geguzin need not have feared for her sons, for Hershel was presumed to be alive and well in New York, while Pina and Yuri had long ago abandoned Vilna for Moscow. Only the Geguzin women remained—mother Hinde and daughters Olga, Fanya, and Ida—and with them Olga's husband and her six-year-old son Emmanuel.

The conscription drive unfolded much like the pogroms of old. Russian troops marched down Vilna's streets, invaded the homes, and carried off the remaining young men—among them Olga's husband. The ostensible reason was to serve in the Russian army. But as in pogroms of old, most of the conscripts, including Olga's husband, were never heard of again. Two generations later, among those whose roots are with the Jews of Vilna, 1914 is still remembered as the year of the czar's last pogrom.

Within a year, the Russian armies were in disarray and the German army was able to occupy Lithuania with virtually no resistance. The occupiers proceeded to dismantle the Russian institutions and set up an ethnic-based government, something the Lithuanians had struggled for and failed to achieve under Russian rule.

For the young widow Olga Geguzin Piore, it was clear that she must remove her little Emmanuel forever from the clutches of imperial Russia. She would take the boy to America—to his Uncle Hersh, whose own departure from home she had never ceased to lament. Olga's image of her americanized brother grew in magnificence as plans for her own departure went forward. Early in 1917, under German occupation, mother and son were able to leave Vilna by train, their land destination neutral Holland. Traveling across German-controlled Poland and Germany itself, they arrived in Rotterdam, only to discover that their ship, which flew the Dutch flag, was not permitted to depart. Wars create many unexpected situations, even in neutral nations. Olga and Emmanuel's voyage to America was delayed six weeks, for the English Channel had been mined by the British fleet.

Olga Piore was the sort of newcomer to America who perceived every problem as an opportunity yet to be defined. She had brought some funds with her, along with a good sense both of business and of neighborhood. She took an apartment at 118th Street and Madison Avenue, which was a fine address in those days, and promptly set up a beauty shop. Over the decades, it would provide a satisfactory living for the mother, and for the son the best education available in New York. All that lacked was Hershel, the lost brother who was surely somewhere in the great city of New York. Olga and Emmanuel would wait, and one day Uncle Hersh would knock on the door. Such was their faith in family.

As it turned out, it would take another five years for this faith to be rewarded. In December of 1922, Emmanuel's Uncle Hersh, whom he had never met, finally rang the doorbell.

4

Americans in Paris

I am an American. . . . I went to England eleven years ago, attended Oxford University for two terms and then went to Heidelberg University, Germany, where I was forced into a duel with a young German nobleman. I killed him. For this I was sentenced to ten years' solitary confinement in a fortress. I do not know where the fortress was. I knew Germany was at war, but I did not know with whom. Six months ago I was released from prison and went to Paris. . . .

I was born somewhere around New York and I went to school there until I was seventeen. I find it difficult to remember anything of my youth now, after so long a solitary confinement in prison. . . . It is hard, very hard, to return to one's native soil and then to be sent to Ellis Island like an alien from a strange land.[6]

The First World War, the bloody war that was to end all wars, finally came to a halt through an armistice signed on November 11, 1918. The winners were the British Empire, France, the United States, which had entered the conflict in 1917, and a host of peoples from various nationalities scattered about Europe. The major losers were the German and Austro–Hungarian empires, which were actually disassembled to create a number of ethnic-based nations. Months earlier, Russia, once an ally of Britain and France, had signed a separate peace with Germany. But that was the least of the changes endured by this once-powerful empire. In March 1917, the Russian czar was deposed. Eight months later, a second, more violent revolution occurred, bringing to power Lenin's version of socialism—radical communism. Under this regime, the Russian royal family was executed along with members of the aristocracy and millions of others who were unlucky enough not to have fled the country. Those who did flee tended to turn up in France, with which the Russian upper classes had a centuries-old cultural affinity.

Thus Paris was awash in refugees from the Russian aristocracy. Too often the mothers arrived alone with their children, for the husbands had vanished either on the wartime front or under the executioner's sword. These remnants of the gentry were generally unprepared for making a living on their own. Yet in many cases, they adapted admirably, serving as translators, giving music lessons and language instruction, hiring out as housekeepers, even engaging in factory work.

In the summer of 1922, an unexpected opportunity unfolded for two of these refugees, both Russian princes who had studied English along with French during their childhood. The place was the American Library in Paris, and the coveted position, hardly considered lucrative in other circles, was that of a shelver—to place returned English-language books in their proper places on the library shelves. To work in this outpost of American culture—not only to sort books but also to read them—was viewed by these penniless Russian émigrés as a golden opportunity.

The library itself was an unintended legacy of the war. During the conflict, the American Library Association had sent to France a collection of some ten thousand books to be distributed to American soldiers at the front, on leave, and in hospitals. By 1918, a central distribution point had been set up in Paris. It immediately achieved an unexpected popularity, not only as a library, but also as a gathering place for Americans and for those who wished to associate with Americans. When the war was over, no one wanted to give it up. Thus, in 1920, the library was incorporated and rededicated as the American Library in Paris, to be supported through an endowment created by the American Library Association. The library was well located, at No. 10 Rue d'Elysee, near the Place de la Concorde, and the building itself, once a hotel, was most beautiful. Funds grew substantially, thanks to the efforts of the American ambassador in Paris and the many Americans who swarmed through the city in those years. All in all, the American Library in Paris was a grand institution in a city that seemed to burst with joy in those first years after the war.

With ample funds now available, a permanent librarian was selected—one Dawson Johnston from the St. Paul Public Library in Minnesota. He assumed his Paris position in November of 1921. Dr. Johnston's library outreach was to extend far beyond the confines of the American community. Under him the library expanded its mission to include all of Paris—not only the French inhabitants but also the many émigrés from across Europe who had found sanctuary there after the collapse of the old order. The American Library in Paris was to become a showcase of America when it came to literature, culture, and history. So decreed the librarian.

Dr. Johnston's concept of outreach included another dimension, that of hiring destitute young refugees who had a smattering of English in their backgrounds. This bit of American altruism became the springboard to opportunity for the two unnamed princes. Unbeknownst to the princes, *they* would become the inspiration for the life journey of the unlikely working companion who soon joined them.

It came about in this way. Soon after hiring the Russians, Dr. Johnston hired a third shelver—one Harry Gerguson,

Oxford educated, polished in manners, and personally modest, as suited the best of the British upper classes. The young man was slight of height with deep brown eyes and quite handsome in a darkly romantic sort of way. In language and knowledge, Harry Gerguson was a match for the aristocracy from any land. Yet he claimed to be an American awaiting repatriation to his homeland!

The young women on the library staff were quick to take notice. Among them was one Dagny Nissen of Minneapolis, Minnesota, daughter of a Norwegian immigrant family. Having finished her university studies, Dagny had come to Paris some months earlier to be with her younger sister Elizabeth, who was enrolled at the Sorbonne. Dagny had taken a tiny two-room apartment on the Rue Leopold Robert and had joined the library staff about the same time that Harry arrived. She was temporarily living alone while Elizabeth traveled in the south of France. Not unlike her colleagues, Dagny found the mysterious American quite worthy of her attention.

One afternoon a curious incident occurred at the library. Two gendarmes of the Paris police delivered to the front desk a sealed suitcase with a tag attached. On the tag was written: HARRY F. GERGUSON. So reported the desk clerk afterward. Harry was summoned to the desk. He signed the receipt, then without a word snatched the suitcase and carried it down to the basement cloakroom. Rumor spread quickly through the entire library staff: Harry, the American, must have just come from prison. How else would the gendarmes be in charge of his belongings? Presumably he was a dangerous man.

Dawson Johnston's wife also served on the library staff, and she was particularly cautious. Harry's presence had created a suspicious situation, she declared—a situation that would require her continuous attention.

Dagny Nissen reacted otherwise. A social worker at heart, she doubted that such a modest young man could ever be considered dangerous. Furthermore, if he had indeed been released from prison, he had already done penance for any wrongdoing. Such a human being ought to be given a second chance. Others might shun this vulnerable young American, but not Dagny Nissen.

One evening she invited him to the cafe where she normally took dinner. Harry looked around and refused to sit down at a table. He could not stand the smell of inferior French cooking, so he said. As a solution, Dagny invited him to dinner in her tiny apartment, five flights up. Harry enjoyed himself immensely. One invitation led to another, and then a third. Within a few weeks it had become an evening ritual. After work, Dagny would stop at the meat and greengrocer shops, then hurry home to prepare dinner for Harry.

Late in September, Dagny's sister Elizabeth arrived in Paris to continue her studies. She observed Dagny's deep concerns over the mysterious American, and she was filled with dismay. Something was amiss—something she couldn't exactly define.

She needn't have worried. Within a few days of her arrival, it was all over for Harry at the library. Mrs. Johnston accused him of stealing a fountain pen—an accusation Dagny swore was false. Taking up Harry's cause, she pleaded with Mrs. Johnston, then with Dr. Johnston, but all in vain. Harry was fired from the American Library, and he no longer came to supper. Yet his library working experience was serving him well. Harry had observed the Russian princes with whom he worked. Indeed they were nothing special, in fact were somewhat boorish in their behavior. And as for being fluent in English—one of the requirements of the library position—well, neither of them could hold a candle to Harry, so he reasoned.

Harry would try out his own Russian prince persona across the Seine on the Left Bank, among the students, the artists, the writers, and all the others who saw themselves as intellectuals. The Left Bank was thick with Americans. What would they make of a Romanoff prince? As it turned out, a great deal, for he became an instant sensation.

On the right bank of the Seine, far from the haunts of struggling young artists and intellectuals, stood the Ritz Hotel. It was a glamorous place, with crystal chandeliers and gilt trim throughout, vintage French decor. Even the bar at the Ritz had gilded furniture and drinks at a price to match. This was the gathering place for Americans blessed with ample funds and unlimited time to tarry. At any given hour on any given day, a crowd of them could be found at the Ritz bar. And by late October, the crowd included the emerging Prince Dimitri Michael Alexandrovich Obolenski-Romanoff, who never found it necessary to pay for his own drink.

Early in November, however, Harry appeared at Dagny's door. He had come to say good-bye. For lack of financial resources, he was forced to abandon Paris and all that was dear to him in that beautiful city. He was sailing shortly for America to make a new life wherever fate might lead him. The Lord willing, he and Dagny might meet one day again. Might he take Dagny's hand in one last fond farewell?

The startled young lady drew back. She bolted to the other room and returned with thirty-five francs.

"Harry, please take this," she insisted. "You will need a winter coat in America."

"Oh, no, I cannot accept charity from you," he protested.

Dagny moved closer and pushed the money into Harry's pocket. He offered no resistance, but bowed deeply, took her hand to his lips, declared his deep devotion to their friendship, and left.

Later Dagny learned that Harry had purchased a pair of stylish spats, declaring them to be a gift from his dear friend Dagny. Dagny shook her head. Would Harry never learn?

Harry Gerguson sailed for New York from Cherbourg on the United States vessel, the *President Adams*. It was a curious group of passengers that occupied third class. The United States Shipping Board had offered free passage to indigent American citizens who for one reason or another were stranded in Europe after the war. They numbered 212, including ex-servicemen hired by the U.S. Government to mark the graves of fallen American soldiers, Belgian and French wives and children of servicemen who had shipped home earlier with their units, likewise widows whose American husbands were killed in the war, and a number of other Americans who had applied for free passage, claiming lack of funds. Among these was Harry Gerguson!

The arrival of the *President Adams* at Hoboken, New Jersey, on November 28 generated a great deal of sympathetic fanfare. The nonpaying passengers who disembarked from third class were met by representatives from the American Red Cross, the Travelers' Aid Society, the New York State Board of Charities, and the Department of Public Welfare. The people of New York were making sure that all the new arrivals would reach their final destinations.

But not all of the 212 were permitted to go ashore so easily, for the assistant commissioner of U.S. Immigration had come on board to examine documents. Eleven of the male passengers could not provide satisfactory proof of citizenship, among them Harry Gerguson. All eleven were transported with their luggage to Ellis Island pending further investigation.

When it was Harry's turn to face the temporary Board of Inquiry, he related a series of misfortunes—his studies at Heidelberg, the duel that resulted in the death of his adversary, a lengthy imprisonment in total isolation, and finally freedom, but with severe damage to his early memories. The Board of Inquiry was not convinced. They would need to look further into the matter, and this would take time.

Harry Gerguson was assigned temporarily to a dormitory on the island. Then, on December 23, he disappeared, along with all of his belongings. This had never before happened on Ellis Island.

5

Prince Dimitri Alexandrovich Obolenski-Romanoff

My mother was a Romanoff and my father an Obolenski. Yes, I trained at Eton and Oxford and served as an officer in both the British and Russian armies. I was still at Oxford when the war broke out. My schoolmates were all going down, so I asked my emperor's permission to fight with them. I was in the Tenth Hussars for two years, when my emperor called me home to command a regiment of Cossacks.

When the revolution came, I carried on until I was arrested for obstructing the work of the people's commissars. I was in St. Peter and Paul prison for eighteen months and then I got away.

I have worked all my life, as hard or harder than the ordinary man, but at a profession that is now unremunerative. My income was, before the war, half a million a year. I had a bit in England and in France. I had many friends, too, and I lived in the old way, for I was sure the dreadful regime in Russia would soon pass. In six months all I had was gone. . . .

I traveled in England, Paris, the south of France, Constantinople, and finally turned to America. I thought I could lecture here and thus make enough to live. But the season was late, and my manager could not get enough engagements to pay. I planned to talk on political subjects, to show what the needs of Russia are. The Soviet agents got busy. I was beaten on the street by thugs, for these Soviet agents wish

*to keep me from speaking against communism. I was not
frightened but my manager was. So I decided to push west.*

   *I must get work in the open. I am hampered in that I
haven't the slightest idea how to go about it. I have been used
to all things coming to me. And now I must search them out.
And it is so hard on my dignity too. . . .*[7]

In early January 1923, Prince Dimitri Michael Alexandrovich Obolenski first came to the attention of the New
York public. The management of the Hotel Belmont had
given him a suite of rooms as temporary shelter until the
prince could find a suitable situation. Prince Obolenski
made it known that in the afternoon he would be available
to the press in his Belmont rooms. New York, like Paris, was
already well populated with Russian princes; yet there was
something about Prince Obolenski that set him apart from
all the others. At the appointed time, the prince's suite was
packed with reporters, many of them quite skeptical, for
bogus Russian princes were almost as numerous in
Manhattan as the real thing. The young man introduced
himself and laid out the many letters of introduction he had
brought with him from Europe. A few were signed by
American expatriates currently residing in Paris—names
both recognized and respected. Others held the signatures
and seals of titled aristocrats, whose countries were familiar,
if not their names. Letters were circulated and examined.
One could sense the sympathy and respect that increasingly
permeated the rooms. The prince's posture and superb
command of the language betrayed his innate self-confi-
dence. Yet in tone and content, he proved to be exceedingly
self-effacing, even as he told of his unusual arrival in
America. The prince began by recounting his humiliating
detention at Ellis Island and explained how he tied up in a
silk scarf his most treasured belongings, attached them to
his walking stick, then swam from the island over to the
Battery, all the while holding the walking stick between his

teeth. Kindly police officers had helped him ashore. Later, immigration authorities would dispute the prince's version, insisting that he had prevailed on a ferry boat captain to take him ashore. But at the Belmont Hotel there were no challengers.

The prince went on to share with his listeners the frustrations that had overwhelmed him these first days in America. He had brought with him ample letters of introduction from the leading financial and commercial houses in London and Paris. Yet New York brokers and business owners refused to believe his willingness to work simply as a bookkeeper or floor sweeper. He would be grateful indeed if the good people of America would just accept him as an ordinary human being who desired nothing beyond the opportunity to earn his way through honest work!

His request to the contrary, New York was not prepared to accept Prince Obolenski as an ordinary human being. *The New York Times* especially wrote lyrically about the prince's Belmont debut. *The Times* even did a background check on the prince and was able to trace his ancestry back to 1365.[8] Together the Hotel Belmont interview and the *Times* report catapulted Prince Obolenski into New York society beyond anything a letter of introduction could ever have achieved. He became the most sought after dinner guest among the city's Four Hundred, and he never disappointed. Routinely he arrived at events a bit overdressed— spats when the night was dry, tails when a tuxedo would do, and most often a top hat when only a homburg was required. These idiosyncrasies became as much a part of the prince's persona as his broad English accent.

The prince was invited to lecture on "Russia, Past and Present" in the city's most exclusive salons, where he was well rewarded financially as well as socially. His command of European history was exceptional—far more comprehensive than what one would expect from a Russian prince, even an Oxford-educated one. Who knows to what academic heights Prince Obolenski might have risen had it not been for his attachment to Royal Yacht pipe tobacco.

It happened this way: While living in London, Harry Gerguson was a regular patron of the exclusive Dunhill's tobacco shop and especially of Royal Yacht, known to be the most expensive pipe tobacco in the world. Over time he had run up quite a debt at Dunhill's, a debt he failed to take care of before moving on to Paris. And unfortunately, in Paris Harry was in no position to purchase Royal Yacht, even if it was available. Dunhill's of London also operated a tobacco shop on Fifth Avenue in New York, and before long Prince Obolenski made his way there to purchase some Royal Yacht. Much to his dismay, he encountered the new manager, recently transferred from London, who remembered his old customer quite well. Word spread through New York circles like wildfire—Prince Dimitri Michael Alexandrovich Obolenski was none other than the American expatriate, Harry Gerguson, who three years earlier had left London in disgrace.

Even before the Royal Yacht affair, Prince Obolenski had been leading a kind of double life. The prince might reign on the avenue and in society, but he was also at home off Madison Avenue as Hershel Geguzin, the long lost brother of sister Olga. His greatest satisfaction in New York had been his luck in locating her. It might not have happened except that in Paris he had finally overcome his youthful family resentment and made contact with his mother. First, he had written and learned that the Geguzin businesses were prospering once again in Vilna, for after the war the city had been made part of the newly reconstructed Poland. Mother Hinde was busily building up the Singer Sewing business; sister Ida was married and had just given birth to a daughter, Nina; and they all lived happily together in the same flat where Hershel was born.

Sister Olga was living with her son in New York, wondering whatever had happened to her brother. So had their mother written to Hershel in Paris. Thus it happened that on December 17, 1922, fresh from Ellis Island, the long-awaited brother finally rang the bell of Olga Piore's flat and swept the astonished sister into his arms.

From that day forward, a bed and clean laundry were always ready at the Piore flat in anticipation of a visit from Emmanuel's Uncle Hersh. The boy, now in high school, adored his fashionable surrogate father, and the uncle like-wise his precocious nephew. Uncle Hersh's visits meant evening tea around the dining table, where he would enter-tain both mother and son with tales of his daily adventures in circles they could barely comprehend. For Olga, these magical interludes were a vicarious escape from her day-to-day responsibilities. For Emmanuel, they were the inspira-tion to succeed, as Uncle Hersh always added—through study and hard work. In just two months, a twenty-two year family separation had all but been forgotten. Olga once again was looking after her unpredictable brother, just as she had years earlier in Vilna. In the intimacy of the little family, it was a time of joy and celebration.

The unmasking of Prince Obolenski, however, put an end to this family reunion, at least for the time being. Harry dealt with it as he had with every personal crisis in his life. It was time to leave New York—this time for the West. He packed his bag, exhorted young Emmanuel to excel in all his studies, then kissed his sister good-bye. The best he could promise was a postcard from St. Louis, Missouri, gate-way to the Great American West.

Harry arrived by train at Union Station in St. Louis on Tuesday, the thirteenth of March, 1923. He registered at the Chase Hotel and, since it was still early in the day, decided to pay a visit to his old home town, Hillsboro, forty miles east across the Mississippi River. It is not recorded how Harry covered the distance, but he was indeed spotted walk-ing along Main Street shortly after noon that day, wearing an English-cut suit, a shirt with standing collar, a wide polka-dot bow tie, pearl-colored spats, and a stiff derby. He strutted into the center of the town square swinging a heavy cane—it was a brilliant sight to behold. Word initially went out that a stranger had come to town, but the true realization promptly followed: Harry Ferguson was back! For sure it was Harry; he still looked like a foreigner from southern Europe, but what a change. In fifteen years, the untamed boy with the awkward Brooklyn accent had been transformed into a perfect English gentleman. Old school friends, now grown, appeared on the street, eager to welcome the hometown boy and inquire as to what he was all about. They invited Harry to dine at the cafe where he had once swept floors, and in spite of all protestations, his money was no good in Hillsboro that day.

Then came the key question: What was Harry doing in Hillsboro? Just passing through and wanting to visit friends of his youth.

Two months ago I was sent back to the United States by the British military department and have been in Washington, D.C., since then. I am now on my way to Tulsa, Oklahoma, in regard to some matters of a government nature. I expect to be in this country about three more months. While on my way to Tulsa, I have a stopover at St. Louis, and as I had a day of spare time, I couldn't resist coming out here to see my old friends whom I remember so well.

I have never married, as my salary is too small to consider matrimony. I have spent considerable time in France, Germany, and Italy and have learned to speak the languages of those countries. I find the French girls too emotional and affected. The American girls are wonderful but are too self-possessed and too sure of their conquests.[9]

Harry asked to visit his old school. Above all, he wished to thank Miss Betty Coale, to whom he owed so much of his success. When he strode unexpectedly into her sixth-grade classroom, taking her hand and raising it to his lips, she blushed so deeply that even the children tittered with embarrassment. Though flustered, she gamely introduced the visitor and invited him to speak. He told the class how he had once gone to school in England, and he described the games the English children played. Finally, he exhorted the class to do better in the classroom than he had done.

By late afternoon, Harry Ferguson was on his way back to St. Louis. The prodigal son had come and gone, but for a few hours it had been a wonderful time for all!

That evening Prince Dimitri Michael Alexandrovich Obolenski was comfortably ensconced at the Hotel Chase. The hotel clerk must have taken note of the distinguished visitor's signature, for the following morning a reporter from the *St. Louis Star* appeared at the hotel to interview the intriguing visitor; the visitor graciously obliged. The reporter first inquired whether Prince Obolenski was indeed a prince.

> *Yes indeed, only where I once was a master of millions—cash and men—I now face the problem of supplying the dictates of my pampered tastes without any visible means. . . . I have been reduced to three things—my title, my blood, and my dignity.*[10]

The prince then told the reporter of his tragic past, just one of the cruel legacies of the Marxist revolution in Russia, and of his firm desire to earn bread and keep through hard work. When it was all over, the reporter suggested an endeavor that might actually bring financial gain to the prince, for his monetary embarrassment was increasingly evident. "Why don't you write of your war experiences?" he asked. The prince demurred: "No, that I cannot do. I would gladly write on political subjects, but *myself*—no."

On Thursday the *St. Louis Star* published the extraordinary exchange at the Hotel Chase. The headlines read:

MAN WHO SAYS HE IS PRINCE HERE FOR JOB
Dimitri Obolenski Admits He Has Nothing Left but His
Dignity and Must Find Employment Until Monarchy Wins.

HIS MOTHER A ROMANOFF, HE TELLS INTERVIEWER
Came to U.S. to Lecture on Politics—Served in British Army
and Later Commanded Cossack Regiment, He Declares.

Printed below the headlines was the full-length column
interview. Back in Hillsboro, Illinois, just east of the
Mississippi, Charles Bliss of the *Hillsboro Journal* read the *Star*
article. So did other Hillsboro readers of the *Star*. Poor
Harry Ferguson—his imagination had run wild again, just
as it had fifteen years earlier. Before the day was out, the
truth had reached St. Louis. On March 17, without apology,
the *Star* published an even longer lead article, including a
portrait of the charming imposter, all under the headlines:

"PRINCE DIMITRI OBOLENSKI" ADMITS HE IS JUST PLAIN HARRY FER-
GUSON OF HILLSBORO, ILL., AND DEPARTS
Man Who Posed as Relative of Romanoffs Unmasked by Visit
to His Old Home Town, Tells Why He Practiced Deception.

*I acquired by hard study an education and culture equal to
that of many men of wealth and position. It became a fixed
idea in my life that my associates must be of equal culture.
Culture usually goes with wealth, and therefore I, being poor,
would of necessity have been forced to associate with people
whose attitude toward life and whose outlook in general was
the very antithesis of my own. How then could I accomplish
my desire? I had the choice of isolation or of assuming a role
which would give me the entrée to the society of people of my
choice.*

*I chose the latter course. I had known of Prince Obolenski.
I learned of his assassination in Russia. I did not think he
would object to a cultured gentleman living a few years of the
life which had been denied him, and believing that a change
of personality would not only satisfy my esthetic tastes but*

would likewise prove amusing and interesting, I decided to take up where the prince had left off. It was not my intention to impose upon anybody in any way.

I did not expect any financial help from the friends I might meet by reason of assuming the role of a prince. All I wanted was friendship and association. Now that I have tried the role and now that it has failed miserably, I am going to Texas and learn cow punching. . . . I shall trade the derby, these spats, and the cane for the things that cowboys wear. . . . [11]

Even a hardened news reporter could not but be sympathetic with the young man's tale. When the evening train was due, the reporter offered the visitor a lift in his automobile; offer accepted. On the way to Union Station, they passed a building under construction. The departing traveler mumbled, as if to himself, "My life is as empty as that structure, as gray as those walls."

On the Fringe
of Society

6

The Harvard Connection

[The prince] is not a criminal; he is a remarkable man. I believe he will go down in history. Perhaps my name will go down in history with him.—*H. Michaelyan, who in 1925 filed charges of fraud against the prince*[12]

Across the state of Minnesota, perhaps across the entire Northwest, the name of James J. Hill spelled power and success. Hill was the man who built the Great Northern Railroad and who made it the catalyst for developing a region that stretched from the Mississippi River to the Pacific Ocean. The Northwest was Hill's empire, and the city of St. Paul his royal city. James J. Hill and his family not only controlled the railroads, they also dominated the mining industry and much of the grain and cattle trade, along with the banking interests that drove all the other enterprises.

St. Paul, Minnesota's capital city, was the seat of it all. The great Hill family mansion dominated the bluff on Summit Avenue, perhaps the longest, most elegant thoroughfare in all the nation. Built of red sandstone, the massive home was purported to have cost one million dollars in 1887. Below the bluff was downtown St. Paul, with Hill's First National Bank, the Hill Office Building block, and a network of charitable organizations, all financed by Hill family funds.

By 1923, both Jim Hill and his wife were dead. The major Hill enterprises were controlled by their second son, Louis W. Hill, who had expanded the family business interests substantially since taking over in 1907. Louis Hill built his own home just west of the family mansion on Summit Avenue. Equally impressive, it was newer, not quite so massive, and more in keeping with the forward look of the twentieth century. Louis Hill's personal passion was agriculture, especially his North Oaks farm, which lay just a few miles north of the city. This was an experimental enterprise he had inherited from his father—three thousand acres of forest and agricultural land, along with stables and a one-hundred-room home, to which the family retreated each summer.

It was at the Louis Hill North Oaks farm that Prince Michael Dimitri Alexandrovich Obolenski-Romanoff turned up in the summer of 1923. Having left St. Louis in March, somewhat in disgrace, he had gone on to Tulsa to seek his fortune in the Oklahoma oil fields. That adventure too bore little success. At this late date it is difficult to surmise what brought the prince to Minnesota. Was it Dagny Nissen, who it turned out was still in Paris working at the American Library, or was it specifically the Hill family mystique? One suspects the latter, for the prince had that special knack of always connecting with "the best" when it came to money and society.

The North Oaks stable master hired the young man who sought work as a stable groom. The prince had boasted of stable experience in England as well as experience with horses in his Russian homeland, and no doubt, with his incredible quick study talent, the prince performed admirably. Legend has it that Louis Hill soon became aware of the Russian prince in the stables. That simply wouldn't do! Prince Romanoff, nephew of the last czar, was soon ensconced as house guest in the Hill summer home.

Just as the Hill family dominated the economic life of St. Paul, so the Weyerhaeuser family dominated the social and cultural life of the city. And just as the name James J. Hill once stood for railroads, the name Weyerhaeuser likewise stood for lumber. Thus it should come as no surprise that when the Louis Hills entertained at North Oaks, at least one of the St. Paul Weyerhaeuser brothers would be among the guests.*

Legend has it further that one Mr. Weyerhaeuser was so impressed with the gifted young Romanoff prince, who had studied at both Eton College and Oxford University, that he offered to enroll him at Harvard University and underwrite his education. One can imagine that the prince was most gracious in accepting the offer. After suitable expressions of appreciation, the prince left North Oaks and moved into St. Paul. He called on the director of the St. Paul Public Library and brought greetings from the former library director—his old employer Dr. Johnston of the American Library in Paris. The director promptly hired the prince to catalog the library's French and Russian collections, a very short career, it turned out.

Prince Michael Romanoff entered Harvard in September 1923, enrolled in the School of Arts and Science. He took up residence first at the Harvard Union, then at the Phoenix Club. He joined the chess club and within a short time brought honor to the University by winning an intercollegiate chess tournament. They would later say of him that though his strategies were reckless, he had the uncanny ability to plan lengthy series of future moves and correctly anticipate his opponent's responses. Prince Michael became the man to befriend among students on campus.**

---

*In 1923, Sarah Maud Weyerhaeuser was a school girl in St. Paul. She remembers well when the Russian prince came to town. "Everyone fell over each other to entertain the prince; such a draw he was. There was so much excitement." [Phone interview with Sarah Maud Weyerhaeuser Sivertsen, St. Paul, September 16, 1995]

**Although the prince's adventures at Harvard and in Cambridge are well documented, it is possible that he was never actually registered. Harvard University archives have no record of his registration, and

Out of his Weyerhaeuser personal stipend, the prince was able to entertain his new friends at the Phoenix with tubs of caviar and cases of champagne. These initial successes merely whetted his appetite to do even better when it came to acquiring a circle of well-placed friends. In October he arranged a most lavish party at Boston's Copley Plaza Hotel. It turned out to be a grand coup, attended by one or another scion of every Boston blueblood family. When the bill came due, however, it was clear that even the generous monthly stipend from Minnesota couldn't make a dent. To cover the cost, the prince was forced to borrow money from his friends, and when these loans were not sufficient, to write checks on New York banks, all of which eventually came back unpaid.

By November it all came tumbling down. The Copley Plaza threatened to press charges, and a fellow student recognized the prince as Harry Gerguson, with whom he had sailed from France a year earlier on the *President Adams.*

The prince's Harvard education was finished. He made a hasty retreat from Cambridge and returned to sister Olga's welcoming apartment in New York. For Olga, every arrival of brother Hersh became a magical interlude in her otherwise hardworking life. For Emmanuel, each return of Uncle Hersh was an occasion for storytelling along with inspired advice—"Manny, you must study well. Where I have failed, you will succeed."

In January, Emmanuel's Uncle Hersh was strolling on one of Manhattan's fine avenues when a U.S. Department of Justice agent stopped him and arrested him on the spot. He was taken to Ellis Island and held for two months while the Immigration Service mounted a full-scale investigation into his past. The one-time prince now claimed to be simply

---

Weyerhaeuser's descendants are doubtful that their grandfather would have financed his education.

Harry F. Gerguson, a New York-born orphan. Late in March he was granted a hearing.

Harry met with Immigration Commissioner H. H. Curran, who held to the Immigration determination that the pretender prince was born somewhere in the Russian Empire. However, since the United States had no diplomatic relations with the Soviet Union, successor to the Russian Empire, any reasonable deportation would likely cost the young man his life. Besides, Curran was taking a personal interest in him. He could see the potential for a useful life, and he was willing to give Harry the chance.

Harry Gerguson was released from Ellis Island on April 3, 1924, but freedom was short-lived. The moment he set foot on Manhattan Island a waiting police officer took him into custody. In hand were extradition papers. Gerguson was wanted in Cambridge, Massachusetts, on a felony charge. Together officer and prisoner boarded the train. The one-time Harvard student was charged with defrauding a fellow student in the amount of $150.

The Cambridge jail was actually not a bad place. The powers that ruled the Boston environs prided themselves that prisoners were well taken care of. When word spread on campus that the prince was back, but in deep trouble, a continuous stream of old friends came to pay their respects, even bringing along some of the prince's favorite food delicacies.

The trial itself was well attended, and the onlookers were not disappointed. When the clerk called for the name of the accused, he rose to his full military stance and pronounced with grave deliberation each syllable of his royal name: "Prince Michael Alexandrovich Dimitri Obolenski Romanoff." It was the high point of the proceedings, for when the clerk asked for the witness, namely, the student who had filed the charge, he was not present, having been conveniently called out of the country. Friends said he absented himself out of sheer embarrassment. A good friend of the prince, he had filed the complaint the previous November in haste and had regretted it ever since. The prince was now a free man.

It was summer now, the season at Newport, Rhode Island. And where the prince had succeeded so well during St. Paul's previous summer season, might he not do even better with New York society? And in his own way he did. The Harvard experience had built an added element into the prince's fantasy persona. He might not be a Romanoff prince, but indeed he was something extraordinary—a gentleman of mystery whose presence was to be coveted by every hostess who entertained at Newport. It was never clear how the prince obtained his invitations, but there he was— exquisitely dressed for day or evening—at every important event. Even the Vanderbilts were not immune. One of the prince's treasured mementos of the 1924 season at Newport was his engraved invitation to a *bal costume* at the home of Mr. and Mrs. Reginald Clay-Vanderbilt.

Back in New York, he was now a connoisseur of art. Presumably financed by trusting investors, he made a trip to Europe, seeking out paintings by the old masters. These were to become the beginning of the "Romanoff Collection," which he would market to wealthy collectors in the United States. In Paris, the prince revisited his old haunts on the Left Bank. Those who might have known him two years earlier were long gone, but an interesting encounter did occur. Years later, the Austrian-born American artist Lionel Reiss would recall a Romanoff prince who stopped to admire his display of paintings along the avenue. The prince's eye fell on the artist's own favorite watercolor—"Ghetto Street in Wilna, Poland."

"I know that street," said the prince, with seeming surprise and delight.

"Oh, did you once live there?" inquired the artist.

The prince hesitated for a moment, then replied impatiently, "Of course not, but some of my underlings were from there." He was gone before the artist could learn more.[13]

As happened too many times in Michael Romanoff's life, his success would be his undoing. In summer the prince visited the Woodstock art colony and became friends with a number of artists and dealers. Among them was one H. Michaelyan of New York, a respected rug and tapestry dealer, for whom the prince agreed to do marketing on commission. This worked for a time until the prince sold a very valuable tapestry for almost nothing and then failed to turn the proceeds over to Michaelyan.

Romanoff was arrested in December 1925 and held at New York's Tombs jail until April of the following year. The accumulated charges were numerous, all having to do with fraud and conspiracy. Neither the guards nor the other prisoners would forget this inmate who always carried a walking stick during the exercise hour. It seemed that the prince's fellow prisoners, who normally would not tolerate "superior" behavior in their midst, were won over by this inmate who never let down his royal bearing. Outside the Tombs, Prince Michael's friends rallied from all corners of the eastern seaboard—oil tycoon E. W. Marland and Alexander Hadden of the Plaza Hotel among them.

Even within the court system, efforts were being made to modify the consequences of a probable conviction. If Gerguson alias Romanoff were to be convicted, deportation would surely follow. By coincidence, the New York City supervisor of probation, one Edmund Collins, had encountered the case of Harry Gerguson several years earlier when he was working for U.S. Immigration. Collins wanted to believe that Harry was born in New York, and in his attempt to prove this, he had made a more thorough examination of the young man's past than had ever been done previously. Indeed he had accumulated a mighty file.

Shortly before Harry's trial was to begin, Collins arranged to meet him in an interview room at the Tombs. It was a room bare beyond words, with an armchair occupied by Collins, a straight chair opposite on which sat the unfortunate prisoner, and a desk between. On the desk lay a large, thick envelope labeled: HARRY GERGUSON, AKA MICHAEL ROMANOFF, ETC. Collins opened the envelope with studied deliberation, retrieving page by page a lengthy dossier that represented Boston, New York, and London. Collins began to read aloud: Serious problems at two New York orphanages, unresolved charges in Boston, arrests in New York, and a curious record out of England documenting theft of a dress shirt, impersonation of a gentleman, incarceration in a jail, commitment to an insane asylum, and finally deportation. Mike examined the documents with amusement.

"You cannot imagine," he said, "that that person is I."

"You know it is, Gerguson," said Collins. "Why not tell me the truth so I can help you? If you were indeed born in New York, as you claim, then why in heaven's name do you pretend to be a dead prince from Russia?"

"Let me explain," said Mike.

Have you ever been in a bare room in a new house with a view overlooking a park? You look at the park and it is marvelous. You look at the bare walls, and you find them absolutely repulsive. They cry for adornment. That is I. I don't lie because I desire to be a crook and a thief, but because I wish to associate with persons whose lives I believe to be adorned. Frankly, I will lie to you as long as you know me. If I told you the truth, I would feel like a bare wall.[14]

For all the friendship and support extended to Michael Romanoff, both inside and from outside the Tombs walls, the pending trial and its expected outcome were more than he could handle. One night Mike systematically cut both his wrists, then lay down on his cot not expecting to rise again. An attentive guard intervened in time. Mike survived and his case did come to trial. Rather than being further incarcerated or, worse yet, deported, he was given a suspended two-year sentence. The hand of Supervisor Collins was clearly visible in the court's leniency toward this unrepentant defendant.

Mike's first act of freedom was to visit the Michaelyan Gallery, presumably to settle his account and make amends with the man who had earlier caused his arrest. In this way has Michaelyan's name gone into history, forever entwined with that of Michael Romanoff.

7

Failed Expectations

*I do not intend to make any defense as to my identity. It is
ridiculous for me to assume any such position. I will say this,
I am not Harry Gerguson and I was not born in Cincinnati.*

*I am a Russian by birth. When a boy I was sent to England
to study. I am a graduate of Eton and Oxford. My home is in
France. As to my birthplace, it is of no interest to anyone. . . .
You may say I neither affirm nor deny that I am Prince
Romanoff. I do not say that I am and I do not say that I am
not.*[15]

This was a curious time in America, later to be known as
the Prohibition Era. Back in 1917, Congress had submitted to the states for ratification a constitutional amendment
to prohibit the manufacture, sale, and transportation of
alcoholic beverages within the United States. By early 1919,
the required two-thirds of state legislatures had approved
the amendment, which then went into effect on January 16,
1920. Subsequently Congress enacted legislation to fund
enforcement of Prohibition, and many states passed their
own prohibition laws so that enforcement might also pro-
ceed on the local levels.

The politics of Prohibition were complex, pitting unlikely
opponents against each other as well as producing unlikely
alliances—rural versus urban, nativists versus immigrants,

conservatives versus libertarians, Protestants versus Catholics, and wage earners versus the endowed rich.

From the beginning, Prohibition didn't work very well, and as the years passed, enforcement was less and less effective, especially in urban areas. After a New York State prohibition enforcement law was declared unconstitutional in 1925, the "speakeasy" era reached its pinnacle. A speakeasy was a clandestine bar that operated like a private club. They were everywhere on Manhattan. One had a friend, one knew a password, he or she—usually he—was identified visually through a peephole. If one was part of the crowd, it was easy to find a speakeasy. If one was not, there was no entrée.

Michael Romanoff drank in a number of Manhattan speakeasies. He was best known at Dan Moriarity's place on East Fifty-eighth Street, where past and present students from Harvard, Yale, and Princeton hung out. His drinking companions carried names such as Mellon, Whitney, and Du Pont. Mike switched easily between his English gentleman and Russian prince personae. The crowd at Moriarity's loved it. He was attractive; he was not argumentative; and he was interesting, a quality sometimes missing in the lives of these pampered young men.

Paul Mellon was a Yale student who frequently came down to New York on weekends. This quiet and agreeable son of the United States treasurer had formed a friendship of sorts with the penniless imposter. In the spring of 1926, Paul Mellon and a friend stopped at Moriarity's between trains. They were on their way to Pittsburgh for the wedding of Paul's cousin. Knowing Mike's pecuniary status, Paul nevertheless casually mentioned that he ought to come along. Paul and his friend later boarded the train alone. To their great surprise, as the train neared Pittsburgh, Michael Romanoff strolled into their car. Of course, Paul invited

Mike to come out to the Mellon house. There Mike joined the young men for a drink and then went on his way, presumably back to New York.*

In the early years of his life, Prince Michael had tried many endeavors. Virtually all of them failed, mainly due to his own lack of sustained interest. The one continuing interest that had brought some success and carried even greater promise for the future was the prince's talent not only for discovering old masters, but also for placing the appropriate value on such works. Even those who had little confidence in the prince's personal integrity respected his incredible store of knowledge and superior judgment when it came to objects of art. Drawing on this reputation, Michael, in the summer of 1926, put together two satchels of paintings and other art objects that he could transport alone by train.

In October, the prince turned up unannounced in St. Paul, Minnesota. Having completed a midcontinent tour that included Tulsa, Oklahoma, and Kansas City, Missouri, he made it known that on the eighteenth of October he would hold court in the lobby of the fine St. Paul Hotel. He intended to call on the St. Paul families he had learned to know so well during his sojourn there three years earlier. Presumably this meant the Hills, the Weyerhaeusers, and their friends. But it didn't all work out as Mike had planned.

*The legend, repeated many times over the years, was that Paul Mellon invited Mike to his sister Ailsa's wedding, that the invitation was rescinded once Mike entered the Mellon home, that in retaliation Mike stole Paul's trunk, and later at Moriarity's showed off a pair of military brushes with gold handles, each inscribed "P.M." Gift from a friend, Mike was supposed to have said, the initials standing for "Prince Michael." According to Paul Mellon, this was just one of the many amusing tall tales that circulated at Moriarity's bar during Prohibition. He never owned a pair of military brushes, let alone brushes with gold handles, and he never owned a trunk. Nor had Mike ever been invited to either his sister's or his cousin's wedding. [Paul Mellon, September 8, 1995]

Someone notified the immigration commissioner in St. Paul, who called on the young man but was not able to find any outstanding order against him. The St. Paul newspapers did the rest—an exposé and veritable putdown of the would-be prince and his art collection.

The following day, the *Minneapolis Journal* was more generous, taking seriously the prince's previous stay in Minnesota, especially his brief tenure at the St. Paul Public Library. It was a vindication of sorts. Chastened by his St. Paul reception, Harry Gerguson turned to Minneapolis. He phoned the home of Dr. Henrik Nissen to inquire of the two daughters he had met years earlier. Daughter Elizabeth answered the phone.

"Miss Nissen, this is Harry Gerguson—remember, we met in Paris. I worked at the library with Dagny. Oh, how fond I was of her!" Elizabeth was cool. Dagny was not in town—technically true since she was now librarian at nearby Fort Snelling and had a room on base.

"Miss Nissen, may I at least pay my respects to you and your family this afternoon? I am currently resident at the St. Paul Hotel."

Elizabeth consulted with her father, who agreed that Mr. Gerguson should certainly come to call.

"Yes, this afternoon at 3:00 for tea."

Harry Gerguson did come to call on the Nissens that day—taking a taxicab all ten miles from downtown St. Paul. He was curiously overdressed, even for Minneapolis's fine Stevens Avenue—wearing a stiff collar, striped pants with spats, and carrying a huge bouquet of hothouse roses. No Minneapolis man wore spats in those years, and hothouse roses were beyond the means of all but a very few. It became a rather strained tea party—Dr. Nissen unusually cautious and Elizabeth intent on not revealing Dagny's whereabouts. When it was time to leave, Harry invited Elizabeth to the upcoming Sunday tea dance at the Radisson Hotel—a weekly affair attended mostly by Minneapolis's high society but open to all. Elizabeth declined, lest she, like sister Dagny, be taken advantage of by the faux prince.

By the following day, Prince Michael—Harry—was gone from the Twin Cities. Compared to an earlier time, this visit had not been a success.

Nor was life much better in New York. December was a terribly cold month that year, and Michael was in poor health. Rumors abounded that he was lacking in both food and shelter, sleeping in the subways and scrounging food as best he could. Indeed the prince was not well, probably suffering from pneumonia and depression as well after his failed tour of the nation's interior. But he was not without food and shelter, for Olga was always there, and in late December so was Emmanuel. Having finished high school with superb honors, he was now a freshman at the University of Wisconsin, on a full scholarship.

"Why Wisconsin?" inquired Manny's dismayed Uncle Hersh.

The headmaster at Manny's high school believed that not just the select eastern colleges should be rewarded with New York's best. Rather the entire nation ought to benefit from the likes of Emmanuel Piore. Uncle Hersh would never understand, but later Emmanuel's exceptional career would more than validate his headmaster's thesis.

Out on the avenue, it became part of the Prince Michael mystique that the homeless ragamuffin would suddenly appear immaculately dressed to dine at the best restaurant, either alone or as guest of a sympathetic friend. Mike never denied these rumors; in fact, he amplified them when appropriate, for his overriding principle of life was never to let on to anyone whence his roots.

The highlight of New York's winter season was the *Beaux-Arts* Ball, organized by the *Beaux-Arts* Institute of Design to raise money for scholarships, with the *Beaux-Arts* member architects creating the environment. In the year 1927, the date was January 28, the place was the ballroom suite of the Hotel Astor, and the staging was New Orleans in 1803 at the conclusion of the Louisiana Purchase. The invited guests—society and the artists—came costumed for the period 1790 through 1810. As was the annual custom, patrons of the event arranged preball dinners, either in their homes or at various hotels. The actual ball began at 10:00 P.M., with dancing until midnight, when the fabled pageant unfolded—promenading delegations of French, Spanish, and American officials from the period, as well as a few left-over lords and ladies from the court of Louis XIV. The incredible spectacle and the setting would all be described in detail the following day by a *New York Times* reporter. He had left the party shortly after midnight to file his story.

Earlier on the day of the ball, Mike Romanoff rose out of his sickbed and made his way to Dan Moriarity's place. His wan appearance elicited great sympathy. The principal topic of conversation, however, was the *Beaux-Arts* Ball, to which most of the drinkers had a ticket, but certainly not Mike Romanoff.

"Go home to bed, Mike," they urged him. Ailing as he was, the prince could not refuse such a challenge.

"Gentlemen, when the clock strikes one, I shall be there in the most magnificent costume of all."[16]

And so he was. At the stroke of 1:00 A.M., Prince Michael Romanoff presented an engraved *Beaux-Arts* Ball ticket at the door and entered the ballroom in a spectacular bor-rowed Louis XVI costume. His grand entrance provided an unexpected climax to the rich pageant—the high point of a magnificent evening that would be well remembered. The following day Mike collapsed on the sidewalk and was taken to Bellevue Hospital. The diagnosis: pneumonia accompa-nied by acute malnutrition. When word reached Dan Moriarity's place that one of their own had been struck down, the regulars kept constant vigil, literally camping out in the hospital corridors.

Over at Moriarity's they were making their own plans for Mike. His kind was not meant for the damp winter life in New York; he should be in Hollywood! At this time, Paramount films owned a studio in Astoria, New York. A regular troop of movie celebrities* moved back and forth between Astoria on Long Island and the West Coast, with Moriarity's one of their watering holes between trains. In early February, a crowd of them, including a well-known producer, sat at the bar and pondered Mike's future. They pooled funds and bought him a ticket to Los Angeles. The producer would accompany Romanoff, paving the way, so to speak, into the magical world of Hollywood movies.

This was the year when motion pictures first carried a sound track. Warner Brothers studio had produced the first successful sound film, *The Jazz Singer*, with New York vaudeville star Al Jolson. Rudolph Valentino was dead, and other of the silent film stars would fade, but Charlie Chaplin, Gloria Swanson, and Adolphe Menjou were about to hit their stride with sound pictures. Within a few years, a whole new generation of younger actors and actresses would join them.

Just imagining the possibilities that lay waiting in Hollywood filmdom was enough to guarantee Romanoff's complete recovery. He was hardly out of the hospital when he boarded the train for Los Angeles, the Hollywood producer at his side.

For six months, Hollywood delivered nearly all that it promised. The prince's benefactor put together a delicious résumé and arranged for publicity photos under the regis-

*Mal St. Clair, Adolphe Menjou, Harry D'Arrast, Richard Dix, and Tom Moore are named in *The New Yorker,* November 19, 1932, p. 24.

tration: "Prince Michael Romanoff, 76 Rue Spontine, Paris, France."

Mike's first break came when a director of Western films read that the Russian was an expert horseman, trained on the Obolenski estate in Poland. He promptly hired him as an extra for the demanding riding scenes. But Mike never had the chance to show off his riding skills, for riding one morning on a bridle path in Beverly Hills, he fell and was injured when his horse was struck by an automobile. But other opportunities also presented themselves. Warner Brothers was looking for an authority on British military life in the Sudan. They hired the prince as technical director, after reading that he had served in the Sudan as a major in the British army. The studio was not disappointed, for the major possessed an incredible memory for detail. If there were any complaints about the Russian prince, these came from the young women on the film set, especially the actresses to whom he gave more than casual attention, some of it unwelcome. Nevertheless, the prince rapidly became an indispensible asset for anyone entertaining in Hollywood society. And as was too often the pattern in his life, success would be his undoing.

One of Hollywood's most interesting characters in those years was Major General Theodor Lodijensky, formerly of the Russian Imperial Guard. He had recently arrived in Los Angeles from New York and was hired as technical director by the Metro-Goldwyn-Mayer studios. The general was an impressive man in all ways. Standing six foot three inches tall, he was incredibly good looking and talented enough to play a variety of Russian character roles in the years to come. In 1927 he was chairman of both the Russian National Society of America and the Trustees of the Russian Church Society, clearly the leader when it came to Russian émigré society.

In Hollywood, Lodijensky was a minor but charming celebrity, the sort of dinner party guest any hostess would covet. Thus the inevitable meeting took place at a film director's summer patio dinner to which both the general and the prince had been invited. The general immediately recognized the faux prince who by reputation continually dogged his footsteps in New York. Lodijensky claimed to have known the original Prince Michael Romanov in Russia, and in fact to have been with the prince when he was killed in 1918.* In New York he was chronically infuriated by gossip regarding an imposter prince, and he had made it a personal crusade to unmask the pretender wherever he surfaced. In spite of these noble efforts, the living Prince Michael had been the one most called upon, at least in New York speakeasy society, to separate authentic Russian aristocrats from the host of frauds who populated the city's refugee circles.

The Los Angeles dinner party ought to have provided the final denouement in the general's crusade. It didn't turn out that way; yet the confrontation would long be remembered by those who were present. Standing a foot taller than the prince, the general positioned himself as to block his way out to the patio. It was the sort of challenge that in Lodijensky's old homeland would likely have resulted in a duel.

"You are not a prince, you are an imposter," he thundered. The responder looked up into the eye of the challenger and replied with a withering disdain.

"It is beneath my dignity to engage in any controversy with a person of unequal station."[17] Romanoff turned around and walked back into the house. A few seconds later, he entered the patio from the garden and began conversing with an attractive young Warner Brothers actress.

---

*General Lodijensky could not have been with Prince Michael when he was killed. This younger brother of the czar had been arrested, along with his secretary, and held in a hotel in the Urals for six months. In July of 1918, both men were taken into a forest and shot by the Bolsheviks.

In the mind of General Lodijensky, it had been a humiliating defeat, one that must not go unpunished. He promptly filed a complaint with the Los Angeles Police Department, and they in turn called in the United States Immigration authorities. Michael Romanoff was arrested and interrogated by the local police. They could find no law that had been broken in Los Angeles. Then he was questioned by an immigration officer, who lamented that their files contained no proof of foreign birth. Without this, Romanoff was not eligible for deportation.

The *Los Angeles Examiner* took up the the frustrated general's cause and published a front-page exposé. The article detailed every mishap of the imposter prince, from his New York orphanage childhood to the infamous Hollywood dinner party. Together it all spelled the death of a Hollywood career. In an interview with the more sympathetic *Los Angeles Times*, Romanoff lamented:

> *I came to Hollywood in an effort to earn an honest living. I have not posed as a prince. But stories purporting to expose me have made it impossible for me to earn a living here. I planned to stay and fight it out, but I can't last much longer. I have worked a few days as a laborer but I am not as strong as I used to be and I can't stand the strain.*[18]

Michael Romanoff was last seen, suitcase in one hand and the other thumb raised, standing at the side of a highway that led east out of Los Angeles.

8

After the Crash

I am going to smash that man in the face the first time I
meet him again. He has caused me enough trouble—for
seven years he has used me as a reference. I met him in New
York, and since then he has been a shadow over my life. He
can't speak a word of Russian. I have spent hundreds of dollars determining for my own satisfaction that credentials
purporting to show him to be of Russian birth are fictitious.
He needs a personal lesson from me for the honor of all real
Russians.—*General Theodor Lodijensky, formerly of the Russian
Imperial Guard*[19]

The autumn of 1927 found the nation in a glow of prosperity. That curious New York speakeasy set in which
Michael Romanoff once thrived was not only prospering,
but in fact engaging in a frenzy of high living. Wall Street
and the stock market had quite suddenly become a game
for *everyman,* and the most reckless among the investors
were gaining the most. It ought to have been an ideal cli-
mate for the return of the would-be prince. Yet the
Hollywood episode, with its humiliating climax, had so
sobered Mike that with all his chutzpa, he dared not show
his head in his old New York haunts.

Instead Mike made his way to the heart of industrial
America, Pittsburgh, Pennsylvania. He had been there once
before, in 1926, for a brief visit at the home of Andrew
Mellon. A year later, Mike had no expectation of renewing

old Pittsburgh acquaintances. Rather, having earlier observed Pittsburgh's booming industries, he signed on as a common laborer in a construction gang. Such an occupation was out of character for Mike, and like previous occupations, it was to be short-lived. A few months later, he was indeed back in New York, obviously in need of hospital care, the diagnosis: broken ribs and other internal injuries. The explanation: a scoop shovel had mistakenly dumped tons of construction debris on him.

Two years earlier, at the Woodstock art colony, Romanoff had acquired a number of interesting new friends. Among them was Rockwell Kent, fast emerging as America's favorite artist. At Woodstock, Kent had issued Mike an open invitation to come to his estate at Ausable Forks in upstate New York. He knew Mike was no prince, but he was quite certain he had been an officer in the Imperial Russian Cossack Division. Rockwell Kent called on Mike at his hospital bed and made arrangements to send him to the Kent estate. Here, among the horses and the many comforts of Kent's home, Mike should not only regain his health, but also act as an advisor when it came to raising horses.

Mike's Rockwell Kent interlude contained curious elements of déjà vu that probably were not recognized at the time. Whereas years earlier the prince had worked in the Louis Hill family stables, only to move into the family's social circle, so too Mike's role at Ausable Forks changed rapidly from that of consultant on horses to Kent household manager. Thus he found himself in a unique relationship with the famous artist. He began to dress like the artist, walk as the artist did, mimic his mannerisms, and above all practice his penmanship. Mike was soon able to produce with ease a very successful "Rockwell Kent" signature. He practiced it by visiting bookstores in neighboring towns, posing as the artist and presenting his autograph on request. It was a most believable masquerade that appeared to bring no disgrace to the artist himself. And unlike many of Romanoff's adventures, it ended with goodwill on both sides.

Romanoff returned to New York with his reputation redeemed. He renewed old friendships, and best of all was reunited with Olga and Manny. Home for the holiday season, Emmanuel was now a junior at the University of Wisconsin and by all accounts a star physics student. Uncle Hersh would have liked to play a financial role in the education of this prize nephew. He would often express this desire and lament at being temporarily short of funds. The thrifty, hardworking Olga would always make light of it— "Hersh, we're doing just fine." During this season of giving, for the first time ever, Hershel bought for his own mother a gift—a pair of soft sheepskin slippers. He mailed them to Vilna, Poland, and may never have learned whether or not they arrived. The slippers did in fact arrive months later, and Hinde would treasure them the rest of her life. In her last years, she would see these slippers as a personal vindication of her role in the exile of Hershel, her youngest child— an act she had committed in a moment of desperation and for which she would never fully shed feelings of guilt.

1929: In America, the year began with uncertainty when it came to economic growth—a recent slump in residential construction and a slight drop in business capital investment. These trends tended to be ignored, for the New York Stock Exchange was experiencing phenomenal growth. Speculation was rampant, and the pool of investors was expanding exponentially. Almost every week the market reached new heights, but it all came to a crashing end on October 24, which in history has come to be known as Black Thursday. That day, with sales of stock greater than ever before in history, the market began a plunge that would continue for the next two years. Before hitting bottom, it would lose two-thirds of its gross value.

The October stock market crash was not the cause of the Great Depression. Rather it was the prelude. Those ruined in the last months of 1929 were mostly the speculative investors and the financiers who had been funding the speculation, and a mighty crowd it was. It is not difficult to imagine the straits in which many of the young men who frequented Dan Moriarity's upscale speakeasy might have found themselves. Many of them worked on Wall Street or in other financial circles. Clearly the end of 1929 was the end of an era when money flowed easily and the foibles of a Prince Michael were not only tolerated but seen as an enhancement to society's ever-flowing gay life.

A time of deflation is never a happy time, and in the first years of the Great Depression, the harsh economic downturn blanketed the entire nation. Like many others, Michael Romanoff scrambled to keep body and soul together. He had a brief tenure as a bondsman, but that soon vanished in the deteriorating economy. After that he found temporary employment with the Luisi Detective Agency, as a specialist in "entrapment." In January of 1931, he was handed an unusual assignment. It involved one Edward Gould and his estranged wife, Wilma. Mr. Gould was an industrialist in Seneca, New York. He had married in 1921 but was now legally separated from Mrs. Gould. She was living in New York City on a generous stipend from her husband. Mr. Gould was dissatisfied with the arrangement. He wanted a divorce, and at that time in New York, adultery was the only practical grounds for divorce. Mr. Gould hired the Luisi Agency to manufacture grounds for divorce by involving his wife in an adulterous situation.

Mike Romanoff was selected as prime decoy in a complicated plan to create such a situation. The execution of the plan unfolded in the following way: First, a stranger phoned Mrs. Gould to say that he had a letter of introduction from a mutual friend living in Paris. He called again and invited

Mrs. Gould to dinner at a restaurant. There by chance they met a friend of the host. This new acquaintance—this friend of a friend of a friend—was a personable fellow, and soon after he invited Mrs. Gould to dinner with one of his women friends. It was this woman friend who finally introduced the unsuspecting Mrs. Gould to Prince Michael Romanoff.

Given an unlimited expense account for the task, Prince Michael took a suite at the Savoy Plaza Hotel on Fifth Avenue. He then arranged a grand party in his hotel suite, a party that included Wilma Gould and a host of his good friends. With a dearth of parties in depression-struck New York, Mike's invitation became a coveted item. His friends and *their* friends arrived in droves. As far back as the prince's student days at Harvard, it was expected that a Romanoff party include tubs of caviar and French champagne by the case. The Savoy Plaza party was vintage Romanoff, and Wilma was more than a little impressed.

The prince gave Wilma an open invitation to visit him in his suite at any time. She invariably found two stenographers diligently at work: one to take dictation, which the prince proclaimed loudly as he paced back and forth across the floor, the other to transcribe his written notes at the typewriter. On one visit, Mrs. Gould found the prince dictating stage directions as he completed an order to turn the great Russian novel, *The Brothers Karamazov*, into a stage drama. Another time she found him on the phone engaged in negotiating a return of the Romanoffs to the Russian throne. Always the prince was agitated and deep in concentration, as if the entire weight of the world lay upon his shoulders. Wilma Gould was becoming very fond of him.

Such a gentleman was the prince, and so attentive when taking Mrs. Gould to tea or to dinner. It was over demitasse at the last of several pleasant dinners that the prince executed his final move. He placed drops of a knockout drug into Mrs. Gould's coffee, then half carried her to a taxi, and finally up to an apartment, arranged for by Mr. Gould's brother.

There the final drama unfolded. It began prematurely with furious knocks on the door. Then followed an angry cry from inside, "Who enters the bedchamber of a Romanoff?" By the time the intruders broke down the door, the prince had locked himself in the bathroom. The raiding party entered the apartment—Mr. Gould, his brother, his lawyer, and a pair of photographers. Fortunately all the commotion caused the unlucky Mrs. Gould to wake up. She found herself lying alone on a bed with no idea as to how she had come to be there.

What was to have been an open and shut case of adultery against Mrs. Gould became a half-million-dollar lawsuit against Mr. Gould's brother, his attorney, and the Luisi Detective Agency. It was a *cause célèbre* in Manhattan, time for Mike Romanoff to lower his visibility. For sure, he did not collect the handsome reward that had been promised him. However, he had embarrassed Mrs. Gould sufficiently so that she was not averse to buying him a train ticket out of town.

Records show that Prince Michael Romanoff, brother of the late Czar Nicholas, spent a few days in Tulsa, Oklahoma, staying at the Tulsa University Club. There he was best remembered for his tales regarding the romantic lives of his cousins, the kings and queens of Europe.

Hollywood memories were short in those years. In March Prince Michael turned up in Los Angeles, once again a royal celebrity. This time he was accompanied by a pet dog, whose name was also Michael. It all began quite well—a separate bungalow at the Ambassador Hotel, dining at the best eating establishments, and a bevy of adoring female friends. At the very fashionable Henry's Restaurant, Romanoff sought out manager Joe Berliner.

"Joe, I owe you $50 and I want to pay you—they didn't give me a chance last time I was out here. I've made

$180,000, and I want to be your friend." Mike wrote out a
$50 check drawn on the Equitable Trust Company of New
York. It would eventually come back unpaid. The manager
would value the check nevertheless—a treasured memory of
an extraordinary man.

The Prince Romanoff masquerade ended abruptly when
General Lodijensky learned he was in town. The general
notified police, who phoned their colleagues in New York.
Michael Romanoff was wanted for questioning in the *Gould
v. Gould* lawsuit. Given that this was a civil matter, however,
the police were in no position to arrest him.

Time for the two Michaels to disappear. In their place
came Rockwell Kent—the famous artist—with his dog
Sport. His first appearance was at the Hollywood Book Store
on Hollywood Boulevard. Wearing a stunning paisley shirt
with an orange scarf, he inquired about books illustrated by
Rockwell Kent. As soon as the startled manager, O. B. Stade,
realized that this was Mr. Kent himself, he produced the
bookstore's guest book for the artist's signature. He had
seen Kent's signature before, on limited editions. Clearly
this example was genuine. He invited Kent to his home for
tea, where Kent was introduced to authors Robert and
Katherine Barrett. They had just completed a book, *A
Yankee in Patagonia,* soon to be published by Houghton
Mifflin. The Barretts prevailed on the visiting artist not only
to illustrate the book, but also to write a preface. Stade, who
had engineered the coup, notified the publisher himself.

For the next few days, Rockwell Kent appeared daily from
12:00 to 2:00 at the Hollywood Book Store. He graciously
autographed books illustrated by Kent while Sport looked
on. The Book Store had become the busiest place on
Hollywood Boulevard.

Of course, it all blew up when a picture of the imposter
Prince Michael Romanoff was printed in the *Los Angeles
Times.* Stade recognized the man he had thought to be
Rockwell Kent. He called Houghton Mifflin to apologize for

the ruse, and Houghton Mifflin notified the real Rockwell Kent at Ausable Forks. So amused was Kent by the charade that he agreed to rescue the Barretts from their embarrassment by illustrating the book and writing the preface himself!

But Sport and his master had vanished for good. The following week, one R. A. Adams turned up in Reno with his dog. He was entertained lavishly by several recently divorced women and quietly left town after paying his hotel bill by check. When the check came back to the hotel unpaid, the embarrassed Adams family of New York made good on the amount.

In June, Mike sailed for Europe on the *Olympic,* having boarded the ship at New York with the first-class passengers and disembarked at Southampton through a service entrance. He is said to have been dressed in a steward's coat and laden with a basket of soiled linen.

9

The Last Great Charade

I thought I could get away with it, but it seems that I was wrong.[20]

Just what motivated Michael Romanoff in this dash to Europe has never been quite clear. The entire continent was plunging into an economic depression that did not distinguish between victors and vanquished from the recent World War. It is not clear what Romanoff expected out of England, nor how he found his way down to Paris.

Paris in 1931 was certainly not the Paris of a decade earlier. The euphoria following victory in the war had been replaced by political instability and a divisiveness within the society that went from the far left to the far right. Still, for Mike, the Ritz bar ought to have been a return to glory. In 1931 it was the regular meeting place of Scott and Zelda Fitzgerald, Ernest Hemingway, Alexander Woollcott, and more—a company wholly suited to the likes of the would-be prince. But it never got to that, for on his first appearance at the Ritz, he was stopped at the entrance. The manager presented Mike with a large unpaid bill dated 1922. Mike prevailed in the standoff by insisting that according to French law, all bills were disallowed after seven years. But the encounter badly tarnished his reputation, for with money scarce everywhere, such shenanigans no longer added to society's amusement.

The prince left Paris and traveled to the south of France. At Cannes he was arrested while staying in a luxury hotel, accused of stealing a checkbook from a wealthy American woman. The police searched the prince's baggage, expecting to find a treasure-lode of stolen merchandise. All they found were soiled clothes and a pile of newspaper clippings covering an entire decade of the prince's adventures. Under questioning, Mike assured police that he was an American. His address: 216 East Fifty-eighth Street in New York City. When the news reached New York and was published in *The Times,* there was cause for great amusement. Mike had given to the French police the address of Dan Moriarity's speakeasy!

Quite likely Mike was detained at Cannes for a matter of months. Afterward he found a temporary home with an American couple who had acquired a chateau near Tours— a chateau much in need of repair. To compensate for his board and room, Mike agreed to repair the plumbing and undertake the seemingly endless job of patching the stucco and stonework. It did not last long, though, for Mike was lonely and yearning for home. He made his way back to Paris and survived for a time on funds gathered through various ruses. This had become a very unhappy episode in his life.

When the French Republic's flagship—the *Ile de France*— sailed from Le Havre on April 19, 1932, Grand Duke Michael Romanoff, heir to the Russian throne, was discovered to be on board.

He had encountered some difficulties on the boat train from Paris, for he was unable to check his two heavy suitcases. Fortunately two helpful young Americans, traveling together, agreed to carry his baggage directly to their cabin when they boarded ship. After that there were no problems. He succeeded in boarding inconspicuously by mixing with the other first-class passengers. Nor were there any problems once at sea. Mike fetched the two bags from the state-room of his new friends and stored them in the dog kennel on the top deck. Thus began a most remarkable sea voyage, no matter that it ended in disaster a week later.

The public unmasking of Prince Michael Dimitri Alexandrovich Romanoff occurred at noon on April 28 when the ship landed in New York. He was marched down the gangplank in handcuffs, followed by an immigration officer carrying a gold-tipped walking stick and two pieces of luggage fetched from the dog kennel. It was a humiliating homecoming, in full view of the passengers with whom the prince had expected to form lasting friendships. Never mind that the famous conductor Arturo Toscanini had been on board and that the son of the great Clemenceau had also made the crossing. Their presence would soon be forgotten by those who had encountered the Grand Duke Romanoff in 1932, on the *Ile de France's* spring crossing.

On Ellis Island the prisoner identified himself as Harry Gerguson, born in New York and orphaned at three years. For those who had been around Ellis Island for a while, the legend of Gerguson's dramatic escape from the island a decade earlier was still alive. At that time, he had had no proof of birth or citizenship; he still had no proof of birth or citizenship—nothing. However, in 1932 the Immigration Service was in possession of a long list of grievances against the young man—the kind of grievances for which deportation was the only choice. Harry was frantic—he demanded the opportunity to appeal. If he were sent back to France, he would immediately be incarcerated—how could his own country wish such a fate on one of its own. Immigration remained firm; clearly Immigration had been too lenient the first time, back in 1922.

By order of U.S. Immigration, Harry Gerguson was to be deported on the French liner *De Grasse*, which was scheduled to sail May 10. The date was still a week away, and the prisoner, rather contrite by now, requested permission to retrieve his worldly belongings from storage since it appeared he would never again see his native land. The director of the Deportation Bureau was moved enough to grant the request. James Drury, a guard, was assigned the task of accompanying the prisoner to Manhattan with the expectation that they would return on the ferry boat that night.

It was a curiously circuitous journey from the ferry boat to Harry's storage locker. Along the route lay a number of speakeasies, at each of which the prisoner felt obligated to make a final farewell. There was great lamentation at every stop and numerous farewell toasts to both prisoner and guard. The climax of the pilgrimage occurred at Dan Moriarity's place, where word of Mike's dilemma had been relayed by telephone. Drinks and more awaited the pair as the gentlemen from Harvard, Yale, and Princeton offered one last salute to their exiled comrade.

James Drury passed out on Fifty-eighth Street in front of Moriarity's. The following day he returned to Ellis Island to report the loss of his prisoner, prompting his dismissal along with that of three others from the Deportation Bureau. Not surprisingly, the commissioner felt compelled to mount an investigation into Ellis Island security. The immediate task, however, was to find the prisoner. The commissioner ordered a stakeout in front of every speakeasy that Drury could identify as having visited. It was hardly necessary. Harry Gerguson was arrested late in the evening on May 9, leaving the building at 315 East Sixty-eighth Street, where he had earlier told Immigration his belongings were stored.

Harry Gerguson was on board the French liner *De Grasse* when it sailed for France on May 10. As the ship pulled out, his face could be seen peeking out from a barred porthole below the brig.

Michael Romanoff's absence was actually mourned in New York circles. And the longer he was gone, the more affectionate the memories of him became. *The New Yorker,* that enduring chronicler of New York life, sensed a vacuum that needed to be filled. Writer Alva Johnston was assigned to investigate the curious saga of Harry and Michael and do a piece on it. Not only was Johnston a more than competent investigator; he was also an uncommonly talented writer. The result was a five-part *New Yorker* "Profile" entitled "The Education of a Prince," published in five consecutive weekly issues beginning October 29, 1932. It was a brilliant piece of writing—accurate to the extent of available sources, irreverent on all accounts, and wonderfully affectionate editorially. The series ended with the November 26 issue, in which the writer gave evidence of his own prescience: "He [the prince] is in jail in Paris now; his friends do not expect him over here much before the night of the *Beaux-Arts* Ball."

10

Return from Elba

It is glorious to be free and it fills me with ambition. My past is behind me. I am struck by the parallel between my case and that of Bonaparte when he left the island of Elba. This is the beginning of the Hundred Days.[21]

Early in December of 1932, the French government wired New York immigration authorities that Harry F. Gerguson was about to be released from a six-month jail sentence in Paris. Arrested in May for vagrancy, he had failed to heed a deportation order, the crime for which the sentence had been levied.

The immigration commissioner took the wire very seriously. Given the Gerguson fiasco in spring and the recent lampoon in *The New Yorker,* much was at stake when it came to the commissioner's reputation. Over a two-week period, he ordered increased security at all shipping docks under his jurisdiction—all docks at the port of New York, and New Jersey as well. These efforts notwithstanding, the published reports beginning December 23 were most painful—the prince had been seen in a midtown speakeasy the previous evening. He was reportedly impeccably dressed in a business suit and claimed to have arrived that day on the North German Lloyd's luxury liner, *Europa.* It had been a comfortable trip, especially dining with his old friend Andrew Mellon, now U.S. ambassador to England. The following day a further sighting—this time at a fine New York restaurant in the company of a prominent lawyer.

The *Europa?* This was Germany's newest and most prestigious passenger liner, built and launched as the nation's challenge to France's *Ile de France.* More than nine hundred feet in length, the *Europa* was measurably greater than the French ship in both size and capacity. The interior design—bourgeois German—was hardly avant-garde, but the ship was indeed elegant in an old-fashioned European way and absolutely dependable as to schedule, service, and matters of security. Thus when gossip of a successful stowaway reached the *Europa's* captain, he took it as a personal insult. The North German Lloyd forbade stowaways; the crew of the *Europa* would not tolerate a stowaway; therefore, there could not have been a stowaway on board. So proclaimed the captain. It was a bit more difficult to put away the claim that the rogue in question had dined with Andrew Mellon. The best the skipper could say was that this too was impossible; Ambassador Mellon had always dined alone in a private dining room.

The immigration commissioner was less certain, though equally on the defensive. When the New York press demanded a statement, he declared:

"I have ordered a thorough investigation of the report that Harry Gerguson arrived in New York City on the *Europa.* Immigration officers are in the city now checking up on reports of his appearance here. From our inquiries so far we do not believe that Gerguson arrived on the *Europa.* If he is in New York, it is possible that he came in some way other than on board a ship coming into the port of New York."[22]

As federal agents fanned out across Manhattan, nervous speakeasy managers issued orders to bar Romanoff at the door. Certainly no speakeasy cared to give the "feds" reason to call. But if the speakeasies were uneasy, the prince certainly was not. The *New Yorker* series had turned New York's favorite "bad boy" into a national celebrity. Mike continued to make his way across midtown, accepting with equanimity any rebuffs, of which there were mighty few, and otherwise finding solace among his growing circle of admirers.

On December 29, Michael Romanoff was arrested by New York police outside Dunhill's tobacco shop on Fifth Avenue, where he bought a new pipe and a quarter pound of Royal Yacht tobacco with a $10 bill. He had shaved off his mustache and was dressed in a tweed cap, fur-collared coat, angora sweater, corduroy trousers, and walking shoes, all topped off by a distinctive multicolored scarf. "Why the winter sport outfit?" asked the arresting officer. "Just back from Canada" was the reply.

Mike may have had intentions of fleeing to Canada; if so, he had tarried too long. But the man most upset by his arrest was Dunhill's manager and Mike's old friend from London, Sidney Ballinger. The Immigration Service had gone to Dunhill's two days earlier, demanding that the police be notified if the fugitive should appear. Ballinger had so informed his employees, one of whom had been the informant. When poor Ballinger learned of his part in the prince's apprehension, he was heartbroken:

"I feel very bad about it. I admire the man because he is a perfect gentleman and I am sure that if he were let alone, he would be all right. He is shrewd, but there is nothing vicious about him. Even after he got some merchandise under false pretenses, we trusted him and sent him his favorite tobacco on credit. When he had money, he paid. If the federal agents had not come here and notified us what to do, we would not have done anything; but under the circumstances we felt honor bound by our sense of duty to notify the police. I've known the man since 1919 and I'm convinced he is an American citizen."[23]

Although Ellis Island was overcrowded with two hundred people being held for deportation, Harry Gerguson was given a small, whitewashed private room. Early in the day his attorney, Alan Salter Hays, paid a visit and found his client leisurely smoking a new pipe. The commissioner had made it clear to the press that if Gerguson's entry on the *Europa* was proven, then the government would ask for the maximum sentence under a law forbidding reentry into this country within a year of deportation. Presumably Hays discussed the matter with his client, but later with reporters he waved away all questions. Rather he chose to announce a contract just signed: Metro-Goldwyn-Mayer had purchased the motion-picture rights to Alva Johnston's series of *New Yorker* articles.* The film studio had also offered Michael Romanoff the position of technical director; he was considering his response.

On New Year's Eve, Mike appeared at his first hearing. He was dressed as he had been at his arrest. New was the tiger orchid pinned to his sweater. The government had done its work well. They had located the original "Gaygussen" file from the Society for the Prevention of Cruelty to Children. It included data corroborating earlier evidence that Harry's birthplace was Vilna, Lithuania. A representative of Manhattan's Hebrew Orphanage was brought in to interview Harry and confirm that he was indeed the child once under their guardianship. There was still no evidence of entry into the United States, nor would the government ever find such evidence, for Harry had entered the United States listed as Hershel Bloomberg, a fact to which neither the Bloombergs nor Harry would ever admit.

Mike's legal representation now included two attorneys—Hays and Tonkonogy—both serving pro bono and intent on proving that their client had been born in the United States. It could easily have come to a deportation order that day, but they prevailed on the hearing panel to hold open the inquiry. It was New Year's Eve, and surely everyone

---

*Metro-Goldwyn-Mayer never made the film, although more than one screenplay was written for it.

wanted to get home early. So relieved was Mike that he exuberantly wrote out greetings to his friends across the bay:

"At my palace on the Isle of Ellis . . . Best Wishes for 1933."

Early in January a special investigator was sent up from Washington to determine Harry Gerguson's citizenship. The immigration commissioner assured all who inquired that the case would remain open as long as there was any possibility of proving him to be an American citizen. Pending the investigation, the government would release the man if sufficient bond were posted. It did not take long for that to happen.

Three days later, an impressive group of Mike's supporters arrived by ferry on Ellis Island. Led by the two lawyers, they included Mike's new agent, his bondsmen, news reporters, and unidentified hangers-on. The bondsmen posted a $2,500 bond and Mike was released. Standing at the boat's bow, he took a Napoleonic stance while recalling Bonaparte's dramatic homecoming. On shore, the party was greeted by a crowd of friends and sympathizers along with a mass of puzzled immigrants.

The freed man walked ashore and proclaimed, "New York! Exhilarating!"

"That's right," chimed the theatrical agent; "Quite true, Mike," added Mike's attorney; "You're talking now," concluded one Sam Mahoney, who identified himself as the prince's bodyguard and representative of the RKO theater in New York.

Mike's inner circle entered a cab for the drive to the Park Central Hotel. Other cabs followed, each filled with passengers who claimed to be close to Mike. Now in home territory, he was absolutely radiant. At the hotel, he went right to a telephone and called his old friend Ballinger at Dunhill's: "This is Prince Michael Romanoff. Listen, I want some tobacco . . ." And indeed, within a half hour, a full pound can of Royal Yacht was delivered to the prince, compliments of Sidney Ballinger.

As predicted by *The New Yorker* magazine in late November while Michael Romanoff was still incarcerated in a Paris jail, Mike attended New York's *Beaux-Arts* Ball on January 20. In 1933, it was held at the Waldorf-Astoria—the theme a fantasy cruise around the world aboard the *Ile de France*, with stops at many exotic ports. Mike arrived shortly after midnight in a full-dress suit, quite possibly the suit he donned each evening on his spring crossing of the *Ile de France*. It would be like Mike to play on the resemblance of illusion to reality. Now viewed as a celebrity of sorts by New Yorkers, he presented his invitation card and entered the ballroom amid thunderous applause.

On his first day of freedom, Mike had signed a contract with RKO theater—a ten-week vaudeville stint for an unheard-of $500 each week. The prince's vaudeville career would be cut short, however, and it might never have been recorded but for Alistair Cooke, that most favorite observer of American life and manners. In January of 1933, Cooke was newly arrived in the United States and tasting the delights of New York. Among his newfound pleasures was vaudeville, still thriving on stage, even as sound movies were fast bringing about its demise.

Alistair Cooke attended a performance of the prince's short-lived vaudeville act, and almost fifty years later, he recalled the event in his delightful book, *The Americans:*

> The orchestra struck up the Russian national anthem, the old White Russian anthem, and a backdrop descended on which was emblazoned the imperial double-headed eagle, and a little squat man waddled out with a toothbrush mustache, jug ears, cutaway jacket, and an uncomfortably high collar. Of course he was a comedian. But then I realized of course he was not. His jug ears were a natural misfortune, his cutaway and four-inch collar were no gag but a strenuous

impersonation of elegance. He was announced by a thun-
derously amplified voice as the son of Alexander III, none
other than His Imperial Highness the Prince Michael
Alexandrovich Dimitri Obolenski Romanoff. There was a little applause and much rustling curiosity, because the audience knew that he was not the last of the Romanoffs but the
first—and certainly the last—of the Gergusons of Brooklyn
to claim the imperial purple and the blood blue.

All I remember about the performance was that it was
weirdly pathetic without meaning to be. He spoke in a
rolling Oxford baritone, in an English much too grand for
the King's English. He told about his experiences at court,
and the audience tittered, the orchestra played again the last
twelve bars of the anthem, and he bowed himself out. He
was, of course, a fraud and he had no performing talent. If
he had been W. C. Fields pretending to be the King of
England, the audience would have been in hysterics.[24]

Later in the essay, Cooke described the faux prince in
more praiseworthy terms, for years later in Beverly Hills he
would come to know well this comic pretender who was
gifted with such "enormous charm."

Surely not more than a day or two after the vaudeville
performance so well remembered by the young
Englishman, a federal grand jury handed down a twin bill of
indictments against Harry Gerguson. The first indictment
was for perjury and false swearing before the Immigration
Board; the second indictment included charges that Harry
had entered the country illegally and eluded federal authorities. Both indictments were in response to the special investigation just completed. Convictions on all counts could
have resulted in a prison sentence of up to fifty-five years.

After much bargaining behind the scenes, the defendant
appeared before Judge John C. Knox and pleaded guilty to
all counts of the double indictment. He was sentenced to
three years in prison and immediately placed on probation.
The government had been more than generous; Harry's
responsibility was to leave the vaudeville stage immediately

and to cease and desist from impersonating Russian royalty or any other persons for the purpose of personal gain. The first was not so difficult—that very day the theater placard was taken down. The second would not be so easy—to abandon Prince Michael Romanoff, the persona that he had in fact become. Mike's final words to the judge said it all:

> I didn't want the vaudeville contract. I was urged to take it. It was a chance to rehabilitate myself, to earn some money, to live in peace and be left alone. It is not vanity [pretending to be a Romanoff prince]; it is loneliness. What is more, I am not lazy. I'd take a job if I could get it. It seems to me sometimes that we are just like ants, milling around and around. But what about? Nothing.[25]

At Home in the
Land of Illusion

11

Good-bye to Gotham

Get him away from Broadway!—*Federal Judge John C. Knox,*
speaking of Michael Romanoff[26]

It wasn't until the summer of 1935 that Mike Romanoff
actually left New York. His last two years in the city had
been unfortunate, and the prevailing economic situation
was certainly a factor. In depression-plagued New York,
there were mighty few in Mike's crowd who could carry him
along. It was more than that, however, and in hindsight a
key culprit in this abandonment was the demise of
Prohibition. Franklin D. Roosevelt had been elected
President of the United States in November of 1932, and
with him the Democratic Party was swept into Congress.
One of the first acts in the new House and Senate was a res-
olution proposing a Twenty-first Amendment to the United
States Constitution, this amendment to repeal the
Eighteenth Amendment—the Prohibition amendment. By
the end of 1933, two-thirds of the state legislatures had con-
curred, which meant that the prohibition of alcoholic beverages was no longer in the federal realm. For sure, in New
York, this marked the end of a peculiar era in which the
temptation of participating in an unlawful but pleasantly
tolerated pastime had created an esprit de corps that did
not recognize differences of age, class, or economic status.
Speakeasy society had been one great brotherhood wherein

a penniless immigrant like Mike could form very real attachments to the rich, the famous, the not so rich, and the not so famous, and consider these attachments the underpinning of his life.

The demise of the speakeasies and the growth of less accessible private clubs certainly contributed to Mike's isolation. But he did have his moments of redemption. He succeeded in winning a bit part in *Say When,* a Broadway musical starring Bob Hope that ran sixteen weeks. And when the motion picture *Catherine the Great* came to New York, Mike himself became a one-night star. The United Artists press agent conceived the idea of featuring the bogus prince—now the most famous of all *living* Romanoffs—at the opening of this film depicting the life of the great Russian empress. Mike was agreeable, but he laid down a number of conditions to be met by United Artists—"a stunning blond, $150 for a night's spending money, a Rolls-Royce with a liveried chauffeur and footman, the footman to wear a tan stovepipe hat, tan coat with gold buttons, scarlet vest, and knee-high tan boots with buff tops."[27]

Conditions were met, and the premiere performance went off with all its splendor. Afterward Prince Michael escorted his blond companion, a well-known Powers model, to the Stork Club and El Morocco, where they supped exquisitely, all the while toasting Mike's royal ancestor. In 1934, a dollar had at least twelve times the worth of a dollar in the 1990s. Thus when the evening was over, Mike still had a mighty $30 left, which he divided between the chauffeur and the footman. Like Cinderella, Prince Michael left his royal coach as penniless as he had entered it.

Michael Romanoff had a curious streak in him—a sense of charity toward those who he presumed suffered the want and indignities he knew too well. To such he could be more than generous without thought for his own condition, while with equals and betters, he found it impossible to see beyond his personal and momentary pleasures.

Early in 1935, the Damocles sword that had hung above Mike for so long finally fell into his pathway. He was called to testify as a material witness in Wilma Gould's $500,000 lawsuit against her husband, his brother, and his lawyer. Edward Gould's divorce petition had long ago been dropped, and he had in fact been declared insane. None of this played into the mammoth civil proceedings, however. For Mike, *Gould v. Gould* became an all-too-painful public appearance, hardly compatible with his growing celebrity status. Subpoenaed to appear daily in court, and without any funds or the wherewithal to earn them, he was locked out of his hotel room for nonpayment of rent.

Mike could always count on a clean bed at sister Olga's flat, although nowadays he more often opted to sleep in the subway. He had made a personal vow never to knock on Olga's door unless he could bring something of value to enliven her own strapped circumstances. In these years, there were mighty few times that Mike came calling at 118th Street off Madison.

So public was Mike's predicament that he was once again placed under federal arrest for "general violation of probation." Judge Knox intervened, as he had two years earlier. Lamenting that Romanoff was a victim of an unfortunate childhood and "a product of our public institutions," he waived sentence on the promise that Mike leave New York permanently.

Fortunately, Mike still had a few loyal friends in Manhattan. One of them, stock broker John Walters, had just bought an abandoned farm at Powhatan near Fredericksburg, Virginia. He invited Mike to move down there and take over as caretaker. Mike accepted the offer, and it turned out to provide a blessed interlude in his fractured life. The place was totally in need of restoration. Mike took hold and repaired the house, cleared a field, and even rebuilt a road. Lacking human company, he acquired a mare, whom he named Betty, and a cat, whom he dubbed Gerguson. For Christmas, he decorated two evergreen trees—one for Betty with a wrapped package of sugar lumps underneath and the other for Gerguson with a beribboned quart of cream beneath. Then he invited his neighbors in for coffee. They were, by turns, both delighted and respectful. They knew that Professor John William Adams of Yale treasured his privacy while on sabbatical here at Powhatan, where he was writing *The Philosophy of History.*

But Mike's seemingly idyllic sabbatical was to be short-lived. When the great Broadway hit, *George White's Scandals,* played in Richmond, Virginia, Mike was there for the opening. He knew everyone in the cast, as well as the producer and press agent. Local reporters became aware of Romanoff's presence, which resulted in the inevitable unmasking of Professor Adams. No longer comfortable among his disappointed neighbors, Mike felt compelled to return to New York.

Back in the city, he was still persona non grata. Sympathetic friends urged him to go west—to Hollywood—to a place more in keeping with his temperament than the surly and depressed East. To ease him on his way, they presented him with a few dollars and a 1933 Ford convertible. No matter that the exterior was somewhat the worse for wear, this would indeed become Mike's golden carriage into the West.

Michael Romanoff turned up in Hillsboro, Illinois, on a Tuesday evening in October 1936. Leaving a mountain of luggage piled on the back seat, he parked his open convertible on Main Street and quietly registered at the Hillsboro Hotel. Nevertheless, his presence was noted, for later the *Montgomery County News* described the visitor's distinctive arrival costume in detail: "A form-fitting, sport-style, gray wool coat with wide red diagonal plaid stripes, gun-metal

Mike Romanoff, portrait by C. F. Foster Studio, Hillsboro, 1936
Courtesy Acme Photos, Chicago, Illinois

gray trousers, and good brown buck-suede shoes. His blue shirt was background for a dark blue four-in-hand cravat, and his slouch felt hat was light gray. His vest was white, with diagonal checks of black."[28]

On Wednesday morning, Mike slept late. He dressed himself in a modest plaid wool suit with blue-and-white striped shirt and slipped on a yellow gabardine trench coat. Then, with knotted briar cane in hand, he walked over to the coffee shop and sat down at the empty counter. There he ordered a hamburger and munched away, seemingly unaware of the crowd gathering outside and the sudden increase in business inside. Only when the newspaper publisher, Clint Bliss, sat down on the stool beside him did the visitor come to attention.

"Hi, Mike, who is paying for your hamburger?"

"Why, Clint Bliss, you are, of course."

Then Mike turned around to witness a mass of friendly faces—faces out of the past—eager to be recognized by the famous visitor.

"Am I responsible for all this?" he murmured. Clearly he was mighty pleased.

A few minutes later, another old acquaintance sat down at the counter—Frank McDavid, the banker with whom Mike had briefly lived those many years ago.

"There's that damned banker friend of mine," he beamed.[29] So it went all the day and the evening. Clint Bliss called the hotel to assure the manager that his newspaper would take care of the visitor's bill. Mike moved on from coffee shop breakfast to lunch at the Elks Club, drinks at the tavern, and dinner back at the hotel, always with an entourage in tow. Nowhere in Hillsboro was he presented a check, for all along Main Street more business was conducted that day than at any time since the onset of the depression. Over at the *Montgomery County News* office the phone was constantly busy and the teletype machine clicking continuously. The national news services had gotten

word of Mike's whereabouts, and Clint Bliss insisted they get
it right.

On Thursday morning, Mike made the rounds of a circle
of well-wishers who had come to say good-bye. He shook the
hand of each man and, with a deep bow, raised the hand of
each lady to his lips—an unexpected gesture still talked of
sixty years later. Then placing his monocle in his eye, with
one foot on the running board, he leisurely autographed
the many cards and papers put forth—*Michael Romanoff*—in
an expansive signature worthy of a prince. He must have
decided that this would indeed be his last time in Hillsboro,
for his farewell words had the ring of finality. Mike
reminded the good citizens of Hillsboro how during his
troubled youth they had never turned their backs on him,
which could not be said of many other places. He wished all
his friends well and begged them not to forget him, for he
would always hold them in his memory. Then he slowly
climbed into the auto while Bob Bliss, the publisher's son,
held the driver's door.

"I say, old chap . . . Robert, I'm a bit embarrassed, you
know. My bankers for some reason or other have my
account rather jumbled. I wonder if you could make me the
temporary loan of something like five dollars for a spot of
petrol."[30]

With that, including the five-dollar loan, Romanoff was
on his way. In the years to come, this visit would take on the
qualities of legend—how little Harry Ferguson, who
became Prince Michael Romanoff, had captured the hearts
of Hillsboro and repaid the loan a thousand times by giving
the town its moment of fame.

12

Hollywood

I started it. I had been looking for [Lebedeff].

[Last week] as I was about to drive away from a nightclub, Lebedeff had said to the man with whom I was talking, "Why do you speak to such trash?" I laughed at him. He jumped on the running board as I started to go, and he hit me in the mouth.

Last night was the first I have met him since, outside a cafe or club. I socked him twice. He tackled me and we were separated.[31]

Mike Romanoff drove into Los Angeles on November 6, 1936, having stopped briefly in Tulsa to make repairs on an auto that by now was barely functioning. It had been five years since Mike Romanoff disappeared from Los Angeles, somewhat in disgrace, after attempting to be both Romanoff and Rockwell Kent simultaneously. He returned now to find a city experiencing phenomenal growth, especially in that northwest corner called Hollywood. The nationwide depression, a malaise that seemed to have no end, was all but missing on the Pacific coast, for much of America was handling adversity by escaping to the "movies." The motion picture industry was absolutely booming, with a dozen major film companies dominating the scene. The era of the great movie stars was at hand, and immense amounts of money were being expended in production and promotion, for which there was no precedence.

On the other hand, Los Angeles often behaved as if it were still a frontier community. Those like Romanoff, who came from the East Coast, would early on discover basic differences. A bad debt in New York might simply be a bad debt, a lesson learned in the mind of the creditor. A bounced check, however, most often would end up in a civil or criminal complaint. Mike Romanoff was not the first, nor the last, to serve thirty days in a New York jail for such an infraction. In Hollywood, there may not have been less tolerance for such violations of trust or of law, but the courtroom was not the place where one settled such grievances, nor those of a more social nature—the maligning of one's female companion or any other perceived insult.

In Los Angeles, fists were the weapon of choice, and curbsides at the best restaurants the preferred combat arenas. During the mid-1930s, the *Los Angeles Herald Tribune* daily reported on celebrity fistfights, especially those outside the Clover Club and the Brown Derby, where such spectacles could be guaranteed a film colony audience.

Mike Romanoff came to Hollywood with the purpose of finding his corner of the motion picture industry. He would have liked most of all to act, but his New York attempts had been so disappointing that he was content to settle in as screen writer and technical advisor. Given his own national celebrity status—the *Los Angeles Times* had covered his arrival with a full-column article—Mike ought to have expected favorable mention when his first screenplay was produced. But that's not how things worked in Hollywood. It took a fistfight with Russian film actor Ivan Lebedeff to give Mike the headlines he craved.

Financially, Mike's situation took an abrupt turn for the better. Shortly after his arrival, an acquaintance had introduced Mike to the Clover Club, a gambling casino on Sunset Boulevard that was much frequented by Hollywood's elite. When word spread that Mike Romanoff was a regular at the casino, it began packing in huge crowds. The management recognized the value of Mike's presence and prevailed upon him to come in at least for part of every evening, with the promise that he would win well from time to time. What worked for the Clover Club also worked for Mike, who prided himself on his poker bluffing skills. He soon contracted with James Oviatt, the best haberdasher in town, to furnish him with an entire wardrobe suitable for his ascending Hollywood position. Mike paid the bill a few dollars each month, and later Oviatt proudly attested to the fact that his customer always paid on time.

About this time a young New York attorney and booking agent made his first foray in Hollywood. His name was Irving Lazar.* One evening soon after his arrival, Lazar was invited by an old friend for an evening of casino gambling. What transpired is best retold in Lazar's own words.

> The Clover Club was practically a Hollywood institution. Moguls and stars went there to play for especially high stakes. I went to look, and, maybe, place a small bet. But the crap games and chemin de fer were out of this world: ten thousand on the line, ten thousand back of the line. I stood in the corner with my hundred dollars in chips and timidly placed it on "don't pass," figuring that if they were going to get anybody it couldn't be me.
> "Put it on the pass line," whispered a gravelly voice with a bit of an English accent. He sounded so authoritative that I did as he said. David Selznick made seven on the opening throw, doubling my money for me.
> "Keep it there and take the odds," the guiding voice urged. I followed his directions for about four rolls. Then he said, "Take your money away." I did, turning from the table with five hundred dollars in chips. "You owe me twenty per-

---

*In the decades to follow, Irving Lazar would evolve into the legendary Swifty Lazar, king among actor and writer agents. The name "Swifty" was coined by Humphrey Bogart, for whom Lazar, on a bet, negotiated three film contracts within a single 24-hour day.

cent," said the man, who, I now saw, was imperious-looking
and impeccably dressed. I gave him one hundred dollars
and asked his name.

"Michael Romanoff."

This encounter began a friendship that lasted thirty
years.[32]

By 1939, Mike Romanoff had appeared in two successful
films: Warner Brothers' *Fools for Scandal,* in which Carole
Lombard starred, and a Paramount film, *Cafe Society,* starring Madeleine Carroll and Fred MacMurray.* In *Fools for
Scandal,* Mike lent his overblown Oxford accent to a
London party scene. One might presume that he played a
similar role in *Cafe Society,* for it was a milieu in which he spe-
cialized.

Mike now had a place of his own, a modest flat at 209
South El Camino Drive in Beverly Hills. He had long since
discarded the unhappy Ford in favor of a Cadillac coupe,
and he was often seen chauffeuring one or another of the
many rising young screen actresses. With a wardrobe to
match, he had achieved true Hollywood status, as viewed by
the tourists who lined Sunset Boulevard and the would-be
celebrities who vied to be photographed in his presence.

It was time now to give back something of value to society,
a token of gratitude, so to speak. Helped by a few friends,
Prince Michael Romanoff threw his first party since the ill-
fated New York affair for Wilma Gould five years earlier. The
engraved invitation was inscribed with an imperial "R" and
signed by twenty-two leading Hollywood personalities:

$$\mathcal{R}$$

To Discharge His Social Obligations, Past and Future, We
Have Received Commands from His Imperial Highness,

*In his lifetime, Michael Romanoff would appear in at least a dozen films.
For a listing, see Index and Guide to Names.

Prince Michael Romanoff, to invite _____
to a buffet supper on Saturday evening, June the 10th, at the
Clover Club. Guests will please bring their own liquor and
fee the servants.

Gentlemen in attendance: Robert Benchley, James
Cagney, Charles Chaplin, Harry Crocker, Cary Grant, Mark
Hellinger, Charles Lederer, Herbert Marshall, John
McClain, Frank Morgan, Jay Paley, Everett Riskin, Edward G.
Robinson, Randolph Scott, Jules Stein, . . .[33]

The Clover Club celebration was a success beyond wildest
expectations. Jules Stein donated a full orchestra, the
Clover Club management provided the food, and the guests
did the rest. Not until 6:00 a.m. did it all break up. His
Imperial Highness left with $100 more than he had brought
to the party, having won considerably at the gaming table.
Asked by a *Time* magazine reporter why Elsa Maxwell,
Hollywood's queen of partygiving, had not been invited,
Mike explained it quite simply: "No phonies."

One might say that in the summer of 1939, Hollywood was
Mike's for the taking: as writer, as promoter, as celebrity par-
tygiver, probably even as actor. Never before had he
achieved such a secure status. What then motivated his sudden decision to leave town?

It happened in a very uncharacteristic way. On August 14,
he submitted his resignation as screenwriter for 20th
Century-Fox studios. He made a slow round of his many studio friends, taking each by the hand and bidding each a sad
adieu. When pressed repeatedly for reasons, the best he
could come forth with was a declaration of his intention to
take up farming in Virginia. Of course, no one believed a
word of it.

The truth was much more obvious, though it might never
have been guessed at the time. Mike's sister Olga was writing
frantic letters from New York. She feared desperately for
her sister Ida and for Ida's family. They still resided in Vilna,

Poland, living in the same flat where Hershel and Olga had been born. But terrible things were happening in Europe, and Hersh must somehow come to his family's rescue.

New York was awash in new immigrants, mostly desperate Jews from Germany lucky enough to have obtained an American visa. Each new immigrant brought along a tragic tale about the Jews—denial of their means of livelihood, destruction of their property, their children's expulsion from the schools, near total isolation, and the threat of worse to come. If that were to be just a German problem, one might not have been so worried. But under Adolf Hitler and the Nazis, Germany was on an expansionist rampage. A year earlier, with the tacit approval of nations who ought to have known better, Germany had annexed Austria and occupied all of Czechoslovakia. Subsequently, pressures exerted on Poland, particularly along the Baltic Sea, were increasingly bellicose—pressures to which no sovereign nation could honorably accede. Olga was frantic with worry for her family. Probably for the first time in his life, Mike—Hershel—felt the same desperate tug. If Germany should invade Poland, the Jews of Vilna would be in gravest danger.

Mike sent Olga a wire of his intentions and quietly boarded the train for New York. He would take it upon himself to obtain visas for Ida's family, whatever the cost. Had there been more time, he might have succeeded, but events were moving too quickly. On September 1, 1939, German forces invaded Poland without declaring war. Two days later, Great Britain and France declared war on Germany, for they were bound to Poland by a mutual protection treaty. In reality, they offered almost no assistance. So overwhelming was the German military might that Poland fell within a month. Still it didn't turn out as Olga and Hershel had feared, for Germany stopped short of conquering all Poland.

In mid-September, Red Army troops invaded Poland from the east. Unbeknown to the outside world, Germany had agreed to leave eastern Poland and Lithuania to the

Soviet Union. Thus, in October, the Red Army marched into Vilna and declared it to be a part of Lithuania. In the eyes of Lithuanian Jews, this was generally seen as a protective measure. Olga and Mike may not have understood it that way, but New York was always a long way from Vilna, and with Europe at war, there was no longer any communication.

The possibility of bringing the family out of Vilna had clearly vanished, but neither was the danger quite so acute as first imagined. For the moment, at least, Germany was not going to get its hands on the family of Olga and Hershel Geguzin. With an eased conscience, Mike could now go home—to Hollywood.

Michael Romanoff's lifelong denial of his roots had affected his behavior in puzzling ways. For instance, once in a New York park, he ranted and raved so against the Jews that he caused a minor riot and was arrested for disorderly conduct. In Hollywood, where Jews and anti-Semitism lived and prospered together, Mike Romanoff invariably came down on the side of the anti-Semites. It was part of his persona—most often viewed as an amusing idiosyncrasy—for few doubted that Michael Romanoff was a Jewish boy from Brooklyn.

After 1939, however, there was a noticeable change. For the first time ever, Mike admitted to having a sister in New York and a nephew of whom he was most proud—Dr. Emmanuel Piore, a physicist with a Ph.D. from the University of Wisconsin! The biggest change of all, though hardly noticed, was one of omission. One could no longer count on Mike for a clever Jewish joke.

13

Romanoffs

I detest the salad trade. If anybody tells me he's on a diet and just wants salad and iced tea for lunch, I tell him the Brown Derby is just up the street and he had better go there. We like to serve expensive eaters, and most of all we admire expensive eaters with good taste. . . . And we do have a few such customers—dear people! Clark Gable always has champagne with everything, lots of it, the best, Perrier-Jouët or Bollinger in double bottles and ice-cold. Or Alfred Vanderbilt; he likes the Russian export Louis Roederer that comes in crystal bottles. It was originally put up that way for my relative, the czar, in transparent bottles instead of green ones so that he could see there was no infernal machine hidden inside. Poor Nicky, he would have liked our food very much.[34]

Michael Romanoff was approaching his fiftieth birthday. He had just finished another round in the court system, where it seemed his past would dog him forever. A year earlier, Mike had been arrested and charged with drunk driving. He had spent the night in jail and pleaded guilty the following morning. Now in Los Angeles on the eve of the Second World War, drinking—even drinking excessively—was just one of the many risky games that people played. When it came to the film colony, the courts and the newspapers invariably looked the other way. A modest fine quietly paid took care of everything. With Romanoff it was different. He might cavort with the players, but he must know that he was not one of them, and as if to prove the point, in charging him, the county attorney brought forth court records covering his entire life. For eleven months, Mike's guilty plea carried the threat of imprisonment and, worse, deportation. His trip to New York while on probation, and his unwillingness to divulge the circumstances of the hurried departure, only worsened the situation. Hardly back in Los Angeles, Mike was arrested for violating probation, brought before the court, and sentenced to sixty days in jail, for lack of $50 to pay the outstanding fine.

It was Hollywood's prince of drunkards, W. C. Fields, its most beloved comedian, who paid the $50 and bought Mike his freedom. Fields could not have known that this would be Mike's ticket to success; Mike hardly knew it himself. While he was in New York, an idea had taken form in his curious, creative mind—an eating place, no less, unlike any restaurant Mike had known. It would be a place that combined the conviviality of New York speakeasy society with the rising tastes of a film society that could afford the very best. He would name it Romanoffs.

Mike could look back on the Clover Club party—twenty-two of his best friends inviting all of their best friends. And what a success that was! Why not find investors, just twenty would be enough if each put in $500—pennies by Hollywood standards. It almost worked: John Hay Whitney and Robert Benchley bought seven shares each; Darryl Zanuck and Joseph Schenck each came in with six shares. Others were Charlie Chaplin, Rex St. Cyr, James Cagney, Humphrey Bogart, and Harry Crocker. All told, Mike raised $8,000, just short of his $10,000 goal but enough to go ahead. Under Harry Crocker's guidance, permits were obtained and a corporation was formed. Mike leased a vacant building on Rodeo Drive just off Wilshire Boulevard in Beverly Hills, and Romanoffs was born. To create the interior, Mike hired a popular architect, Douglas Honnold, but the results turned out to be more Romanoff than

Honnold. Later the architect would recall with amusement the tribulations he encountered in designing the original Romanoffs:

> Being the royal architect is an education in itself. I learned more about human vanity at the old stand at 326 North Rodeo than I could have from all the philosophers of antiquity.[35]

Romanoffs was scheduled to open late in 1939. As opening night drew near, Mike was frantic. He was running out of money, and he had no credit anywhere. Not one to skimp when it came to either food—two menu items—or liquor, Mike spent his last dollars on silverware from a hardware store and borrowed enough money to make change.

The opening, on December 18, was sensational, and after that things only got better. The mercurial rise of Romanoffs in Beverly Hills was one great continuous show that no one cared to miss. For the film colony, especially, it was as serious as it was fun. By design, the front area consisted of a curved art deco bar along the entire wall, with five round booths for dining lined up along the opposite wall. The back area was the main dining room, with seating for 170. Perhaps it had not been planned that way, but it turned out that Hollywood careers would rise and fall on the five booths opposite the bar. Mike considered it his personal responsibility to determine who sat in the booths—those to be seen—and who would do the seeing. For sure, the latter included parties drinking at the bar while waiting for a table in the back room. They also included the majority of diners who walked past the booths on their way to tables in back.

In a community such as Hollywood of the 1940s, where visibility and recognition were qualities to be valued above all else, the five booths at Romanoffs were society's qualifiers, and the man who controlled the booths its arbiter. Mike Romanoff fulfilled his role with perfection. He could be imperious; he could be gracious; he might be cutting, or he might exude warmth. But Prince Michael was always in charge, and he had an uncanny sense of position when it came to the ebb and flow within the film colony. Hollywood knew it was all a game with Mike; yet Hollywood wanted to believe in him, and Mike considered it his royal duty to perform accordingly.

And it wasn't only Hollywood that wanted to believe. The New York crowd, especially those from Broadway storming the film studios, were quick to look up the place of the legendary Prince Michael. One such newcomer was actor Hume Cronyn, already well established in New York theater. He made it a point to call at Romanoffs the moment he arrived in Hollywood.

"We've met before," offered Cronyn as he shook the hand of the host. "I once bought a pipe from you—a Dunhill."

So profound had been the first impression made by Mike Romanoff that the actor could still remember the encounter in vivid detail. It was in the early 1930s, at Harry's Bar in Paris. Young Cronyn was in Europe, presumably to study the theater. One evening in this famed watering hole he met the young man known thereabouts as Prince Romanoff. Standing next to each other at the bar, the two men exchanged a few words.

"You're an American of course," began the unlikely prince.

"Close, I'm a Canadian," Cronyn responded. The conversation meandered on until Prince Romanoff remarked that the Canadian was smoking a Dunhill pipe. Would he care to buy another?

"It's a good pipe," the prince claimed, "—almost new, Dunhill of course. You see, I have no money, not a bean." When young Cronyn asked the price, the prince was all humility.

Exterior of Romanoffs, 326 North Rodeo Drive in Beverly Hills
Courtesy Bison Archives/Marc Wanamaker, Los Angeles

"Would five dollars seem excessive." For the well-to-do young Canadian it was not excessive. Hume Cronyn did indeed purchase the pipe for five dollars and paid for the prince's drink as well.

Now in Hollywood almost a decade later, it was Mike's turn to be expansive, for he too remembered this encounter out of his unsettled past. On that first dinner at Romanoffs and on many dinners to follow, word would come down from the top, "Mr. Cronyn, tonight you are Mr. Romanoff's guest."[36]

Romanoffs' first full year was 1940, and it turned out to be profitable far beyond anyone's expectations. The two major investors, Benchley and Whitney, were so undone by the restaurant's success that they early on signed over their shares to Mike. This was supposed to be a gag, not a profitable business enterprise. Later other investors would also bow out, either giving back their shares or selling them to Mike at cost. It would have been rude even to give the impression of sharing in the prince's limelight, let alone in his profits. With more funds available, Mike hired a French chef out of New York. Dating back to his own far-flung youthful adventures, he valued good French cuisine above all other gastronomical constructs. The wine cellar likewise gained a reputation for quality—the best on the Pacific coast when it came to French wine. So Mike would proclaim.

Abroad in the world, however, dark times were becoming ever murkier. By 1941 Mike could not have escaped thinking about his family in Lithuania. His mother had died in 1935. It is difficult to surmise how much this son might have grieved at the time, or whether he had grieved at all, for so many years had passed since he left home. Nowadays "family" at home in Lithuania meant sister Ida, just two years older than Mike. Before long, he would have much to grieve over when it came to this playmate of his youngest years.

Ida Geguzin Marshak was the daughter who stayed at home and cared for her aging mother. Ida married Simon Marshak, and they had two children—Nina and Michael. Grandmother Hinde had lived out her life in their home, her presence considered more a privilege than a burden. Years later, Nina would recall a most happy childhood when a steady stream of visitors came to seek advice from Grandmother Hinde, the wise woman of Vilna. Nina would suppress other experiences out of her past—tales too dreadful ever to bring to the surface—from the time during the Second World War when Vilna and all of Lithuania were in the hands of Nazi Germany.

Germany's invasion of Russia, predicated on conquering the lands between, commenced on June 22, 1941.

The bar at Romanoffs
Courtesy Bison Archives/Marc Wanamaker, Los Angeles

Historians would later debate what prompted Hitler to turn to the east and take on the might of the Soviet Union when Nazi Germany had most of western Europe and was close to defeating Great Britain. On the streets of places like New York and Hillsboro and Los Angeles, Americans puzzled and cautiously hoped that these two evil empires might be locked in mortal combat and go down together. What lay ahead, especially for the Jews, would not be known across America until much later—not to Olga Piore in New York; nor to her son Emmanuel, now a lieutenant in the United States Navy; nor to her brother Hershel in Hollywood.

In 1939 Lithuania had a population of 170,000 Jews, half of them living in Vilna. Less than 10,000 survived the war. What had become of them all? A handful—five hundred in all—had been lucky enough to obtain visas abroad before the Soviets closed the borders. Another group, Jewish intellectuals numbering some 6,000, had been deported by the Soviets to Siberia along with other Lithuanian intellectuals.

When German troops conquered Vilna on June 22, 1941, 20-year-old Nina Marshak had already disappeared "into the forest." Having won Lithuania's top gymnastics award, she was now training underground as a paratrooper and radio operator—her role to be that of intelligence officer behind German lines. For three years, Nina would fight a grizzly guerrilla war with the partisans, but she would survive. For Nina's mother and father and brother, it would be otherwise. According to German records, always carefully kept:

> From Operational Situation Report 21, July of 1941, SS Einsatzgruppe B reporting from Vilna: "The liquidation of the Jews is under way, with five hundred Jews shot daily. . . . Lithuanian police units are instructed to take part in the liquidation of the Jews. . . . They arrest Jews, and put them in concentration camps where, on the same day, the Jews are shot."[37]

Such was the fate of Simon Marshak, husband of Hersh's sister Ida and Nina's father. He was arrested outside his home in Vilna, taken to a place of execution, and shot that very day. Yet five hundred a day was not good enough to clear Vilna of Jews as the German timetable demanded. In organized mass roundups, the remaining Jews in Vilna were taken to the village of Ponar and ordered to excavate large trenches. One hundred at a time, they were lined up naked along the edges and shot from the back so that the bodies would tumble forward. Line upon line, thousands of Jews within a single day met their fate at the trenches of Ponar. These would include Ida Geguzin Marshak and her only son, Michael. By November 1941, Einsatzgruppe B could report that there were no Jews left in Vilna. Across all of Lithuania, only those well hidden in the forests had survived.

On December 7, 1941, Japanese forces bombed Pearl Harbor in Hawaii and attacked other American bases across the Pacific. The following day, the United States declared war on both Germany and Japan. America was at war across the entire land, and virtually every young man wanted a part in it.

By the dozens, the young men of Hollywood's film colony volunteered for military service. Those best known were often set apart to be used for war effort films and other patriotic duties. If there were one or two who chose to stay home and protect their careers, these were identified and shunned. In the rush of civilian patriotic fervor, Mike Romanoff was leading the charge. Whether it was the tug of the Geguzin family strings or simply the call of the Romanoff legend, Romanoffs of Beverly Hills threw the first Russian Relief celebrity event in Hollywood. No one knew exactly where and how the funds would reach the embattled Soviet Union, but that didn't matter. It was one glorious evening. Later in the war, Romanoffs staged a second grand celebrity event, this one netting a bundle for the American Red Cross. These benefits may well have been the first in the line of ever-popular celebrity fundraisers that as yet has seen no end.

Flattered and fawned upon, courted and confided in, the prince of Romanoffs in all ways remained his own man. He lived alone in a flat across from the restaurant and claimed that Mr. Confucius, his English bulldog, managed the household. There was not one man in all of Los Angeles whom an outsider could identify as an intimate friend of Mike's. Nor was there any such woman. Before he opened his own restaurant, Mike was often seen at one club or another, escorting any one of a number of minor film beauties. After Romanoffs' success, those days were over. The best Mike could do was bother his "cigarette girls"—those shapely young women in crisp scanty uniforms who peddled cigarettes and other sundries from table to table. What success he had with any of them was never revealed.

Then along came Gloria.

14

After the War

After all these years as a bachelor, I finally took the big step. I hope I'm not setting a bad example for all the rest of the Hollywood bachelors. . . . We've known each other four years, and we've been talking about trekking to the altar for at least eighteen months. . . . We'll have a honeymoon later. Right now, I've got to get back to work. *

For Nina Marshak of Lithuania, the Second World War ended on July 13, 1944. As communications officer with the partisan army, she was operating her radio in a forest, some thirty miles from Vilna. Over the radio came the message: "Partisans, attention: Vilna fell to the Red Army today; tomorrow, we march into the city with our units." Nina could hardly believe the message, so isolated were the guerrilla units from the front lines. But march they did. On July 14, hundreds of partisans—no, a thousand—came out of the forests from every direction, on foot and in every imaginable kind of vehicle; Nina was among them. Dressed every which way and proudly wearing wide red sashes, they walked eight abreast into a city of rubble. Fifty years later, Nina's memories would focus on the endless columns that passed them in the other direction—more than a thousand captured German army and SS troops being marched out of the city to some unknown fate.

*Just after his Las Vegas marriage to Gloria Lister.[38]

It would be another year before Hersh and Olga in America would learn just who of their siblings had survived. Remarkably the three who had gone to Russia years earlier still lived, each with a tale to tell. Only Ida had been killed— she the playmate of Hersh's childhood who had stayed home to care for their mother. Once Hersh learned that Ida's daughter Nina had survived, he vowed to see her in this lifetime—a living leaf grown out of his childhood roots.

No matter that Vilna had fallen to the Soviets, Germany and Japan were far from being defeated. The best that could be said was that both Axis powers were on the defensive—fighting unsuccessfully to hold onto lands and islands captured so easily in the first years of the war. Many American lives would still be lost in this last year of the Second World War.

Out in Hollywood, heroic war movies and romantic comedies were now being turned out by the dozens. And in between films the best-known stars, especially the singers and dancers, traveled to Europe and the Pacific Islands, performing for the troops on makeshift stages. It was an incredibly hopeful time in America.

At home there were minor discomforts to deal with. Gasoline and certain foods were rationed, other foods simply unavailable; yet money was plentiful. Cafes and restaurants became leisure-time locales where one could order from menu items simply not to be seen on grocery shelves. Especially at Romanoffs in Beverly Hills, patrons still feasted on imported caviar and superb filet mignon. It would have been considered rude to inquire of the proprietor whence came these delicacies.

In this summer of 1944, two young ladies, each barely twenty years old, came out to Los Angeles from the East— Gloria Lister and Cornelia Bailley. They were good friends, off on their first adventure away from home. How they happened upon Romanoffs in Beverly Hills is not known. From Mike Romanoff's point of view, it might have happened as follows: His office was in chaos, his accounting system in disarray, the Los Angeles County rationing board peering down on him, and along came two comely young ladies who claimed to understand numbers and promised to put Romanoffs' books in order. Mike hired them both.

Hersh's nephew Manny—Navy Lieutenant Emmanuel Piore—was stationed out at China Lake, doing his part in planning the invasion of Japan. It was a highly secret operation, but weekends were sometimes free. With Gloria and Cornelia on his payroll, Mike began to entertain at home— in his flat across the street from the restaurant. At weekend parties, Mike's greatest pleasure was turning the hostess duties over to Gloria and playing the "uncle" part as he presented to his celebrity friends the handsome young man in Navy whites, "my nephew, the lieutenant." Fifty years later, Manny would recall that it was always party time in the flat across the street, with Gloria and Cornelia in charge while Uncle Hersh stood aside and smiled benignly.

A year later the war was over, and everywhere across America it was homecoming time. Romanoffs was the scene of one emotional reunion after another. Whether it was buying drinks at the bar for an actor still in uniform or arranging an elaborate party of a hundred for the likes of Cary Grant and Jimmy Stewart, Romanoffs was the place to entertain. And if Romanoffs wasn't large enough, rent a hall and have Mike Romanoff cater the event.

Romanoff of Romanoffs was demanding of himself and equally demanding of his employees—now numbering ninety. Mike boasted that his kitchen was all French. The waiters, on the other hand, came from every corner of the world. Los Angeles was overflowing with refugees, and they turned up daily at Romanoffs looking for work. Mike firmly denied that there were humanitarian considerations in his hiring; outsiders would view it otherwise.

Gloria and Cornelia were totally responsible now for keeping the books. Their boss arrived each morning punctually at 9:00 A.M. He began the day by going over the chef's order for food and liquor, adding or deleting as he saw fit. Mike never let this aspect of the business out of his personal control. Whatever might be reported in the press about the magic of Romanoffs, Mike knew that ultimately business must rise or fall on quality. Mike was generous in allowing regular patrons to charge; he was unyielding in his insistence that charges be paid promptly. Mornings he could be seen writing by hand dunning letters to those whose accounts were past due.

A half hour before noon, Mike made his morning stroll through the kitchen, tasting, cajoling, and acknowledging, without begetting familiarity. His was a carefully developed exterior—to be respected and a mite feared. Mike's entrance into the bar and dining areas would occur only after the maitre d' had sent word to the kitchen that sufficient tables were occupied. Mike would straighten his tie and check himself in the mirror. Then with a flourish, Mr. Romanoff would emerge through the double swinging doors.

In these years, all of Hollywood was divided into two camps—those favored by Louella Parsons and those allied with her archrival, Hedda Hopper. Both women were nationally syndicated Hollywood gossip columnists. A booth assignment at Romanoffs might predict the rise or fall of a film personality, but either of the Mesdames Parsons and Hopper could make or break a career in Hollywood simply with an appropriate word in her column. Both entertained at Romanoffs; both were courted by others at Romanoffs.

And it was at Romanoffs that a much-acclaimed event involving these two celebrated women took place. It happened this way: Hedda Hopper had devoted an entire column in praise of a film in which Louella Parsons's daughter appeared. So pleased was Louella that she phoned Hedda to say thank you. She went on to suggest, "Let's make peace."

"Okay. Name the date and place."

"Let's do it publicly. Say, at Romanoffs tomorrow, one o'clock."

"You're on." And so it happened. Mike reserved the No. 1 booth for the ladies. Hedda arrived first. Moments later, in walked Louella. From all the other booths came requests for telephones. Friends called friends, and before long, mobs of people began arriving, until they were six deep at the bar. All the while the two famous columnists chatted amiably and picked at their cracked crab. Two hours later, with the bar still packed, they rose from the table and left the restaurant arm in arm. It was a wonderful peacemaking, but it didn't last.[39]

In the fall of 1945, *Life* magazine sent a photographer and a reporter to Los Angeles. For two days they camped out at the the fabled Romanoffs. The result was an entertaining article entitled "*Life* Goes to Mike Romanoff's Restaurant."[40] Coverage began Friday noon with host Mike Romanoff in a business suit. He strolled past the bar, where people were still waiting to be seated, paused to greet the regulars in the booths, then turned to tackle the main dining rooms. The restaurant could seat 170, but on this autumn day so soon after the war, the place was overflowing.

George Sanders and Sir Cedric Hardwicke were seated in a sunny corner of one section. Mike visually assessed the customers and the staff, then made his way to their table and sat down: "I say, Sir Cedric, you seem to have a cold; let me order my special hot toddy for you."

"No thanks, Your Highness, I just returned from London, where *everyone* has a cold. It has to be that infernal rain—one entire week and not a single ray of sun. Just give me a day or two of Pacific sunshine and I shall once again be myself."

Ah, yes, London in the rain. That brings to mind a November day in your fine city. It was quite some time ago, November 1918, I believe, the day after the Armistice was signed, that war to end all wars. Oh, what abominable weather we had that day. I had come down to London with some of the Oxford crowd—you know, I did once have connections there. We were all standing pressed together on the great parade grounds opposite Buckingham Palace. It was cold and it was rain-ing—a drizzle without end. Why they could not have signed the Armistice in August I shall never know. At least then one might have counted on a sunny day to celebrate.

But not to disappoint this mass of loyal subjects, the king and queen appeared on the balcony, the king in his dress mil-itary uniform and the queen in her god-awful hat. Well, you know how polite those damned English are—as if on order, every single umbrella in the crowd was promptly closed. But the rain didn't understand; it just kept coming down.

Then the king raised his arm in a salute while the queen pulled out her handkerchief and waved at the crowd. So we all pulled out our handkerchiefs and commenced waving back. We waved and we waved and it rained and it rained, but then the most curious thing happened. The queen began to sneeze; she sneezed and she sneezed and she sneezed; then it started in the crowd—to the left, to the right, behind me and in front of me. Those stupid English sycophants were all sneez-ing—not only sneezing but blowing their noses as well.

I have always thought of this event as just one more demon-stration of that peculiar British trait, a mindless loyalty to their damned monarch. My dear Sir Cedric, may you soon find complete recovery in this blessed land of ours.

Darryl Zanuck and Virginia Fox, his wife,
hosting a party at Romanoffs, 1945
Courtesy Bison Archives/Marc Wanamaker,
Los Angeles

Leaving the two Englishmen muttering in amusement,
Mike excused himself and made his way out to the terrace.
Three boys had just hopped a garden wall intent on getting
the autograph of Van Johnson. It seemed incumbent on
Mike at least to pass the time of day with Johnson's dining
companion. On this day she was Gretchen Donahue—"wife
of Socialite Woolworth Donahue, ex-wife of John Randolph
Hearst." Back inside, Monty Woolley was eating in lonely
splendor at his regular table between the bar and the
kitchen door. The maitre d' had clamped a lamp to the bar
so that Monty might have light, for he always had a book
next to his plate. Even at noon Romanoffs required jackets

with ties. No male patron—not even Howard Hughes—was so important that he would be permitted to violate this cardinal rule. With Hughes, Mike had once showed his displeasure by simply turning him away.

Friday night Mike was host again, this time dressed in a tailored white jacket with black bow tie. He was described as tablehopping in the main dining room. (At Romanoffs only the host—Mike—was allowed to tablehop. A patron observed moving from table to table would find "no reservations available" next time he or she phoned the restaurant.) Gregory Peck and producer Casey Robinson shared a table for two. Mike stopped to make a suggestion as they selected from an elaborate cart of French pastries. Later he consented to join actresses Jeanette Macdonald and Fay Wray, sitting between them opposite their escorts.

I see you are all drinking Chivas Regal this evening. My darling Jeanette, did I ever tell you about the first time I drank this heavenly Scotch? . . . It was in New York, at Moriarity's place on 58th Street. Now Dan Moriarity served only the best, even during Prohibition. We used to go there on Saturday afternoons, when all the college boys were in town—mostly Yalies, for New Haven was not that far away. My connections, you know, were rather at Harvard, but we all got along well.

It was a glorious Saturday afternoon in May, though you might not have noticed in that dark smoke-filled room that passed as Moriarity's place. We took claim to the table from which one could view the comings and goings, for one never knew when the feds might invade. To my right sat a young man from Yale, whom I knew rather well—you would recognize the name if I told you. He was engaged to be married to a very proper young lady from one of the women's colleges. They often came down together. But here he was, in spring, squiring a dandy redhead who for sure was not from one of the seven sisters colleges.

Well, Yalie explained to me that he and Prudence—his betrothed—had agreed to study all weekend, on their respective campuses, rather than go down to New York. He further confided that he could still ace his exams, and that the redhead was just a bit of extracurricular diversion. Yalie was in an expansive mood and he ordered Scotch for our entire table— Chivas Regal, of course.

Such flavor, such body! In all of my travels I had never tasted the likes of this fine old Scotch whiskey. Yalie might have ordered us a second round, but at just that moment the door to Moriarity's flew open and sunshine streamed in. Through the blue smoke there emerged an apparition that I almost dare not describe—Yalie's fiancée Prudence in the company of a young man who was clearly not from Yale. In fact, he looked very much like Moriarity's night bartender. Blinded by the sudden darkness, the unlikely couple was headed straight for our table. You can imagine the scene: seven generations of New England propriety facing the ultimate test. I felt it my duty to diffuse what might become a most unfortunate confrontation. I therefore left my seat, walked right up to the young lady, and looked her in the eye.

"Prudence, my dear, you look fully prepared—for your exams, I mean." The terror in her eyes subsided. I took her hand and raised it to my lips.

To my astonishment, her fiancé, young Yalie, promptly came to my side. I released her trembling hand and retreated. The young man then seized both of his fiancée's hands and declared emphatically: "My darling Pru, I too am well prepared. Meet my ancient history tutor, Miss Maggy um . . ." The blushing redhead nodded her acknowledgment, excused herself, and was out the door. Nor was the night bartender to be seen anywhere. I believe he was hiding behind the bar. Prudence took the vacant seat next to her betrothed while I, as evidence of my conciliatory role in the affair, ordered a round of Scotch for the entire table—Chivas Regal, no less.

*Would you believe that last month Prudence and her hus-
band came out to Romanoffs to celebrate their fifteenth wedding anniversary. I recognized them immediately and ordered
up three Chivas Regal on the rocks. We drank together to that
Saturday afternoon in May, now so long ago; oh, it was a
touching moment . . .*

*Joseph, another round of drinks for a table that seems more
than reconciled—Chivas Regal on my tab.*

After bestowing a kiss on the proffered cheeks of both
actresses, Mike excused himself from a table still basking in
the glow of his brief presence. He must move on to greet
Constance Bennett and Donald Nelson.

The five booths opposite the bar, fully occupied as they
were by tourists from out of town, saw little more than the
back of the host this evening. To be seated in one of the
booths was honor enough; a personal visit from the host
might have been viewed as cloying.

Saturday night meant private parties, large and small. *Life*
found Elsa Maxwell entertaining Darryl Zanuck at a dinner
for fourteen. Contrary to his custom, Mike Romanoff was
dining as one of the invited guests. He wore his customary
white dinner jacket and squired dinner partner Mrs. Joseph
Cotten. Elsa Maxwell's guest list also included Monty
Woolley, Virginia Fox Zanuck, Lauritz Melchior, Esme
O'Brien Sarnoff, Gregory Peck, Mrs. Charles Boyer, Anita
Colby, Cole Porter, Mrs. Artur Rubinstein, and Spyros
Skouras. So reported *Life* magazine, in the expectation that
readers would be as awed by Romanoffs' patron list as was
the reporter.

Los Angeles reporters, and readers as well, were less awed
by film celebrity names than were their eastern counter-
parts. What tickled the Hollywood locals most was the clever
putdown—often meant as a token of affection that flattered
the victim as much as it did the purveyor. Such was the aim

of the *Los Angeles Times* reporter who dialed the phone number of "Confucius," listed at an address across the street from Romanoffs restaurant. It was a gentle jab at Mike Romanoff for believing he was so important as to have an unlisted phone number.

"Hello, is Confucius there?" the reporter began.

"Confucius?" came the reply in a falsetto voice. "Just a minute."

A few clickings of the phone and the deep, accented voice of Mike Romanoff came on the line. "This is Mr. Romanoff."

The reporter again inquired after Confucius.

"I haven't seen him lately. Really, he keeps quite aloof."

The reporter challenged Mike. "What is your dog's number doing in the telephone book?"

"Why, my friend, where else would you expect it to be?"

"Does he get many calls?"

"I suppose so. However, I seldom discuss the matter with him. I just live with him—sort of a valet—you know how English bulldogs are. One thing I know. Confucius is of the confirmed opinion that the average telephone call is not worth answering."

"Smart dog," agreed the reporter, now enjoying the exchange. "Does he get much mail?"

"Oodles. He appears to be apprised of every new refrigerator and vacuum cleaner on the market. Somehow he has established an excellent reputation for domesticity."

"Well, Mr. Romanoff, when can I talk with him?"

"I really don't know when he will be in to the press. But if you care to leave your number . . ."[41]

Mike Romanoff was at home in every sort of voice, including falsetto. His reputation had been made with the well-developed Oxford English intonation. Yet when occasion demanded, such as a visit from a Soviet delegation, he could add a most convincing touch of the continent and mischievously serve up "Strawberries Romanoff" for dessert.* On rarest occasions, he was even heard to slip back into the Lower East Side brogue, a faint remnant of his New York childhood. But to speak in the language of his original homeland—never!

Over the years, Mike's ability to deliver an accent on demand landed him a number of minor speaking roles. In 1947 he played in *Arch of Triumph,* starring Ingrid Bergmann and Charles Boyer. Among all the films in which Mike appeared, this was his favorite.

Always it was Gloria Lister who kept it going at Romanoffs when Mike was off on an acting adventure. Mike couldn't say enough of her beauty, at the same time addressing her as "my Girl Friday" when in fact she was the business manager of a good-sized corporation. Gloria no doubt had an accommodating personality, but she also possessed a strong sense of her own worth. Surely something had gone amiss in the relationship, for in the summer of 1947, with no warning whatsoever, Gloria resigned. Mike was devastated. It had never occurred to him that he might lose her, or that she was even dissatisfied. One can only guess how seriously Mike tried to dissuade Gloria, for asking one's pardon and making amends did not come easily to him.

Gloria may have had her own agenda. She certainly was not without friends. When the wealthy Dolly O'Brien invited her to Florida for the winter, as secretary and companion, Gloria was quick to accept. It was a tough winter in

---

*"Strawberries Romanoff" was a specialty of Romanoffs restaurant. Probably invented by a French chef, it became peculiarly associated with the Russian Romanov rulers. At Romanoffs in Beverly Hills, this haute cuisine dessert called for confectioner's sugared strawberries marinated in cognac and Grand Marnier, soft vanilla ice cream mixed with whipped cream and layered with the strawberries in individual stemmed dessert glasses, all topped with the marinade-juice mixture.[42]

Myrna Loy with Mike Romanoff, 1948
Courtesy Bison Archives/Marc Wanamaker,
Los Angeles

Romanoffs' office, and spring was no better. Assets and cash
flow were not Mike's strong points. Then quite suddenly, in
early February, Mike flew off to Florida. One can only surmise that he had missed Gloria terribly all those months
and quite likely dared not ask her to come back without
offering something beyond what she had before.

These many years later, it might never have been known
that Mike Romanoff was courting Gloria Lister in Palm
Beach, Florida, had it not been for Winthrop Rockefeller.
This youngest son of John D. Rockefeller, Jr., was considered
the most eligible bachelor in the country. On the thirteenth
of February, *The New York Times* broke the story of
Rockefeller's pending marriage to one Barbara Sears—

later, Bobo Rockefeller. The hastily planned wedding was to take place that very night somewhere in Florida. It was only after the wedding that the location and guest list were made public—a midnight marriage at the Palm Beach home of socialite polo player Winston Guest, witnessed by fifty guests, including the Duke and Duchess of Windsor, the Marquess of Blandford, and "Prince" Mike Romanoff of Beverly Hills.[43]

Gloria did return to California, and on the Fourth of July, 1948, at 10:00 in the evening, she and Mike flew off to Las Vegas in a chartered plane. They were married after midnight by a justice of the peace. The bride gave her age as twenty-four; the groom gave his age as forty-eight. In truth he was ten years older. Witnesses were the plane pilot and the manager of the hotel in which they spent the night. By the next evening, the couple was back in Los Angeles. Queried a reporter from the *Los Angeles Times:* "How does it feel to be married?"

Answered Mike, "I don't know—rather frightening, I think. This is a new role for me, you know. But it's really nothing unusual."

"Wasn't it rather sudden?" continued the reporter.

"Oh, no, we've been thinking about it for some time. We just took advantage of the holiday for the trip, and we flew because I had to be back to work tonight."

"Then you've been keeping the secret for quite a while?" the reporter persisted.

"Well, you know I've never been too talkative about anything."

"What about a honeymoon?"

Mike pointedly concluded the interview: "I can't. Have to work, you know. Maybe later. And after all, marriage is primarily a private affair."[44]

In truth, Gloria and Mike Romanoff never did have a honeymoon.

Newlyweds Gloria and Mike Romanoff, July 6, 1948
Courtesy *Los Angeles Times* Photographic Archive,
University of California, Los Angeles

15

Romanoffs II

No conceivable privacy of any sort is possible to any of my patrons. A soup stain on Jack Benny's waistcoat at one end of the room is instantly and graphically visible to Humphrey Bogart at the other extremity. Nunnally Johnson even brushes his hair before coming in to dinner; that's how formal we are in this place. *

From the beginning, there were design problems with Romanoffs—problems increasingly exacerbated by the restaurant's growing popularity. The booth limitation was causing severe and unnecessary friction. There were just five booths, which were parceled out according to a set of rules known only to the proprietor and his maitre d'. It was all beginning to work against Mike, especially on Mondays, when Romanoffs' only true competitor, Chasen's, was closed. Beyond this issue was an uncertainty that might any day turn into a problem. Romanoffs was in a leased building, the lease renewable every five years or so. Mike had already run into difficulties with the two women who owned the property. After the war, he had done a major remodeling that included a new, more regal entrance. The lessors filed suit, attempting to evict him for violating their lease by making changes to the building; Mike barely prevailed.

*Speaking of his new restaurant.[45]

139

He was in a position now to afford even bigger changes. Mike concluded it was time to take complete control by owning his own place. He purchased a piece of property, still on Rodeo Drive but south of Wilshire Boulevard. In 1950, south of the boulevard was considered passé or worse, but Mike was undaunted. He cabled Alfred Vanderbilt, a crony from his earliest Hollywood years: "Send money for a new restaurant—$25,000 will do." Vanderbilt was in Honolulu, but he wired back promptly. Mike should meet an incoming plane the following morning. There would be an envelope on board. And so there was, with a check for $25,000 and a note from the sender: "This is the least I can do for my emperor."

Mike promptly hired architect Douglas Honnold, promising him more freedom than allowed with the earlier restaurant. Still, the exterior and the circulation design were genuine Prince Michael. Three marble steps would lead up to the front entrance, and on the plain facade "Romanoffs" would be spelled out in large stylized wrought iron letters, with the signature royal "R" topped by a crown. An elaborate bar forward as in the old restaurant, for this layout had more than proved its worth. Then an archway and a short flight of steps, creating a grand entrance into the main dining room. Such was Mike's intent. The dining room was to be hexagonal: round padded booths fitted along all six walls and two additional sections of booths in the center, twenty-four booths in all. "No conceivable privacy . . . ," promised Mike.

On October 24, 1950, the cornerstone was laid amid great ceremony. The building site was ringed by a dozen American flags interspersed with the flags of all the United Nations. Comedian George Jessel presided, which guaranteed a liberal dose of irreverent and risqué banter. Ethel Barrymore trimmed the mortar around the cornerstone using a gold-plated trowel. Prince Michael himself tossed a clay effigy of Joseph Stalin, head down, into the concrete

Laying the cornerstone for Romanoffs II: George Jessel,
Ann Miller, Prince Michael
Courtesy *Los Angeles Times* Photographic
Archive/University of California, Los Angeles

under the front steps—a gesture of filial loyalty to "my late cousin, the czar." Afterward, under a green awning, cinema celebrities by the dozens gathered for drinks: Clark Gable, Joseph Cotten, Jane Wyman, Ann Miller, Ronald Colman, Robert Cummings, Bruce Cabot, David Niven, Larry Parks, and more. For Mike, this was the best of halcyon days.

Over the winter, Mike concentrated all of his attention on the building project. Whether it was a big decision or a small one, never mind the architect, it was Mike's decision.

Still, Romanoffs had to be managed, and it was Gloria's turn to show her mettle. She took on the entire responsibility of overseeing day-to-day operations. For the employees, it was no longer the unpredictable Mr. Romanoff with whom they concerned themselves, but rather the cool and efficient Mrs. Romanoff, very predictable and, yes, more feared.

In January Michael Romanoff, the recognized dean of restaurateurs in Los Angeles, was invited to speak to the *Societé des Gentilhommes Chefs de Cuisine*—a collection of prominent amateur male chefs better known in their roles as Hollywood film stars. Much of Mike's message to the group is lost to history, but the climactic words were duly recorded:

> *Everyone I know likes food. Few know anything about it. As soon as they are old enough to go to a restaurant alone, they order fried beans, fried potatoes, or fried eggs. By the time they can afford it, they go to the better restaurants, and what do they order? Steak with fried potatoes.*
>
> *Believe it or not, I started out as a farmer. The farm was going broke, so I came to Hollywood and sold a story to the movies to pay my debts. To celebrate the sale, I went to the finest restaurant, paid an enormous amount, and the food was atrocious. So, like everyone else who has failed at other businesses, I opened a restaurant.*
>
> *To open a restaurant, you know, you don't have to be Greek or Italian, or even a questionable Russian like myself.*
>
> *You must have a good chef, however. There's nothing more useless than a cook who can't cook. The average cook repeats himself over and over like a broken phonograph record. Actually the work requires a great deal of imagination. A restaurant owner doesn't need to be a chef to know that he's getting good food.*
>
> *As Johnson said to Boswell, 'I can't lay an egg, but I'm a better judge of an omelet than a hen.*[46]

Mike might have added, "and there's no chef like a French chef," for at Romanoffs, there was no kitchen unless it was an exclusively French kitchen.

At the beginning of April 1951, Romanoffs on North Rodeo Drive was closed. Mike planned a farewell party for the old restaurant, the climax to be a bonfire in the center of the terrazzo floor. He invited a number of friends to take part, all to the accompaniment of good food and drink. This was to be a sentimental farewell. Mike's dress was always impeccable, but for this occasion he outdid even himself. With a carefully coifed crewcut and smartly trimmed mustache, his benchmade shoes polished to perfection, a fresh formal shirt hand pressed and flown in from New York (Mike always sent his laundry to New York; he claimed they didn't know how to press properly in Los Angeles), a newly tailored white jacket—all in all perfect formal evening dress— the host looked to be larger than his slight five-foot three-inch frame.

Mike had occasionally imbibed too much in his earlier years. It was a habit picked up during Prohibition, when one took all one could get at a speakeasy, for no one knew when the next shipment might come in. As a successful restaurant owner, Mike drank in measured moderation. However, on this final night of the old Romanoffs, he began the celebration early—a martini before the first guests arrived, then another martini with the first guests, and another, and another. Early in the party, he simply passed out on the floor. One of the waiters loaded him into his automobile and drove him home (now a grand Beverly Hills residence at 708 North Beverly Drive).

The farewell "burning" at Romanoffs took place on schedule but without the host. It was a great disappointment—to the employees as well as the guests—and above all to the absent host. Mike took it as a bad omen, for he was inclined to view adversity as a portent of worse to come. He needn't have worried.

Even before the new restaurant opened, the South Rodeo Drive location was moving from passé to preferred. Along Rodeo Drive, on the pathway to the new Romanoffs, there suddenly appeared new shops hoping to cater to Romanoffs patrons, above all, Dunhill's of London with its stock of Royal Yacht tobacco. Dunhill's would not be disappointed.

In early May, Romanoffs reopened at 140 South Rodeo Drive. It was a magnificent edifice of terrazzo and marble with gold-plated fixtures and leather upholstery, all decorated in black and gold. Built at a cost of $400,000, the restaurant had a capacity of 1,000. The main dining room, smaller than the old restaurant, seated just one hundred. Off to the side, however, were the private dining rooms, including the Crown Room with a magnificent crystal chandelier. On the second floor were the larger party rooms. Above all of these was the garden penthouse. To hold a party in the penthouse was a privilege that Mike granted only sparingly. Unfortunately, it was this juxtaposition of a public restaurant with a penthouse accessible only to the chosen few that would later play into Romanoffs' undoing.

From the moment Romanoffs II opened, it was packed, day in and day out, from noon into the evening. And never mind that in these postwar times, the Soviet Union had moved from ally to Cold War enemy. Mike's elegant Russian persona still played with the customers. By this time, everyone ought to have known that the owner of Romanoffs was other than a Romanoff prince. Over the years, Theodor Lodijensky and Ivan Lebedeff had done their best to discredit him. Both film actors had been born in the Russian Empire, and each one resented Mike's usurpation of the Romanoff name. Yet most of the Hollywood crowd wanted to believe, and in spite of repeated unmaskings, many continued to believe.

Romanoffs II at 140 South Rodeo Drive
Courtesy Bison Archives/Marc Wanamaker, Los Angeles

One of Mike's greatest fans in these years was Oleg Cassini, a true Russian aristocrat. During the Revolution, Cassini and his parents had fled Russia, and from the late 1930s he was Hollywood's most acclaimed costume designer. In 1950, Cassini went out on his own with Oleg Cassini designs, which soon became the classic in women's fashions. In those years, Cassini traveled in the Hollywood film crowd. For a while, he was married to actress Gene Tierney, and later engaged to be married to Grace Kelly. Like most of the Hollywood crowd, Oleg Cassini was attracted to Romanoffs as much by Prince Romanoff as by the restaurant fare. He viewed Prince Mike's public persona as a superbly acted character part. He was always onstage, ever amusing, and never offensive. At Romanoffs Mike would invariably greet Cassini as one would a fellow aristocrat of equal rank—bowing ever so slightly while looking the count straight in the eye. In return, the count would address the faux prince in the Russian language, well aware that Mike knew not a word of Russian. This little exchange always played the same. Mike would gently hold up his hand in protest: "No, no, my dear Count, I am completely devoted to this country, which has given me so much opportunity. I wish now only to speak English." Decades later, Oleg Cassini would fondly recall this little charade and speak with great affection of the man who called himself Prince Michael Romanoff.

The mystique of Romanoffs in Beverly Hills was fast becoming of nationwide interest. Early in 1954, *Holiday* magazine sent a reporter out and prevailed on the maitre d' to divulge the names on a random midweek reservation list: a full house with Jack Benny, Jane Wyman, William Haines, Pamela and James Mason, Paul Douglas, Mrs. David Hearst, Mrs. Leonard Firestone, Jennifer Jones and Anita Colby, Hedda Hopper, J. Edgar Hoover, Clifton Webb with his mother, Maybelle, Artemus Gates, Sam Goldwyn, the Cole Porters, and a host of other lesser lights.[47]

J. Edgar Hoover? He was director of the FBI and would eventually serve under seven United States presidents. Over the decades, he had built the FBI from a scandal-ridden presidential embarrassment to a thoroughly professional and unrelenting department of criminal investigation, an agency to be as feared as it was respected. Hoover's private life was the stuff of speculation. A bachelor, he lived a seemingly spartan, monastic life in Washington, D.C. Yet he traveled a great deal, especially to California, where he unashamedly basked in the company of the rich and the famous, particularly when it came to film society. In Beverly Hills, Hoover usually stayed at the home of Dorothy Lamour while squiring the mother of Ginger Rogers about town. His favorite eating place was Romanoffs: "Here the phony tinsel is stripped away and you can see the real tinsel."[48]

Hoover didn't drink, and he was always on a diet, but he was captivated by the Prince Michael persona. He also found wicked pleasure in taking lunch or dinner across the room from the likes of Frank Sinatra and Bugsy Siegel, two of the many personalities on whom his agency kept files. Once at Romanoffs, the notorious gem thief Swifty Morgan approached Hoover, who was engaged to be married. Morgan offered to sell him a bracelet. Hoover examined it and offered $500. Morgan snatched it back and complained, "Five hundred? Why, John, there's a five-*thousand*-dollar reward out for this!"[49]

It can be said that J. Edgar Hoover, beginning in the early 1940s, was the first major government figure to consort publicly with Hollywood entertainment figures. He would certainly not be the last, for in the years that followed, from U.S. presidents on down, Hollywood, New York, and Washington would increasingly connect in strange and wonderful ways.

Not the least of those from the East Coast establishment was Walter Winchell of newspaper and radio fame. His daily news columns from New York commanded a reading audience far beyond all his competitors combined. His evening news broadcasts were equally compelling. Walter Winchell was a veritable kingmaker, a man who could make or break a political career. He hated bigotry, whether directed against Jews, Blacks, Italians, or immigrants in general. In the 1930s, he had railed against those in high places who refused to see the reality of Naziism in Germany. After the Second World War, when the nation's love affair with the Soviet Union turned sour, he directed his tirades against those who refused to recognize the underside of communism.

Walter Winchell always felt close to J. Edgar Hoover, and like Hoover, he reveled in his access to Hollywood society. In the 1950s, Winchell was frequently seen in Beverly Hills,

With party hostess Mrs. Reese Milner, 1953
Courtesy *Herald Examiner* Collection/Los
Angeles Public Library

especially at Romanoffs restaurant—source of the best in Hollywood gossip. Not that any of this could be gleaned from Romanoff himself, for Mike kept confidences like no one else. Rather it was the patrons, many of whom could hardly keep their mouths shut, especially when it came to Hollywood "Red-baiting."

For a time, Winchell was the journalistic mouthpiece of U.S. Senator Joe McCarthy, an unfortunate relationship that would eventually sap Winchell's influence and destroy his career, even as alcohol would destroy McCarthy himself.

Joe McCarthy had been among the first politicians to find Romanoffs II the ideal place for working lunches and dinners. In 1951 he came out to Hollywood to investigate the alleged communist connections in all of filmdom. Joe McCarthy could find a communist anywhere—the better known the person, the more likely that McCarthy would ferret out some connection, real or imagined, to communism and agents of the Soviet Union. In the film industry it was a terrible time. One's career could be ended in a moment if his or her name should appear on one of McCarthy's lists.

McCarthy's Hollywood investigations were conducted under the sponsorship of his Senate committee. Much of the investigating was done through guilt by association. There were people in the community who did not hide their attraction to Marxism or to our old wartime ally, the Soviet Union. It was their friends and associates at whom McCarthy took aim, and for these investigations he had with him Senate staff investigators Roy Cohn and David Schine, along with Robert Kennedy, a young attorney in the U.S. Department of Justice.*

During the Hollywood investigations into communism, McCarthy and his staff were seen daily at Romanoffs. Eating in the main dining room, the foursome was always on display—to the fascination as well as the intimidation of the better known patrons.

Robert Kennedy must have liked the place, for in the decade that followed, Romanoffs could expect members of the Kennedy clan to stop by several times a year. In the summer of 1959, Senator John F. Kennedy invited forty for dinner in the penthouse—a "working" dinner, briefcases and all. With a guest list that included Stewart Alsop and Averill Harriman, it smacked of an early start in Kennedy's successful bid for the presidency. In hindsight, it couldn't have pleased Prince Michael more.

*A decade later, Robert Kennedy would head the Justice Department, as U.S. Attorney General under his brother, President John F. Kennedy.

But back in 1952, Mike Romanoff was an avowed Republican, although he always talked like a Democrat. In the presidential election, Darryl Zanuck and Sam Goldwyn were strong supporters of Dwight Eisenhower; they were also strong supporters of Romanoffs. As a gesture to these longtime friends, Mike agreed to place Republican literature on tables in the main dining room. The gesture turned out to be a serious mistake, for in Beverly Hills these were "McCarthy times." Whatever Eisenhower's credentials might be, he was running under the same party banner as Joe McCarthy. Romanoffs patrons deserted in droves, always to Chasen's up in Hollywood, much to poor Mike's dismay.

Missing the final "burning" at the old Romanoffs had not been the bad omen Mike once presumed. The fallout from the 1952 presidential election, however, suggested an ill wind in the making. Of this, Mike was not unaware.

With Friends Who Mattered

16

Citizen Mike Romanoff

I like Romanoffs because it's the only place to go. I like Mike
very, very much. He is a very entertaining, interesting, and
kind man, a civilized citizen. I can meet friends here. It's
kind of like a club.—*Humphrey Bogart*[50]

In the 1950s Humphrey Bogart was king of Hollywood. He
was married to Lauren Bacall, and they lived in a posh sub-
urb of Los Angeles known as Holmby Hills. Bogart—
Bogie—lunched regularly at Romanoffs, and he always
occupied the second booth on the left off the entryway—
Table No. 1 it was dubbed. When she was not working,
Lauren Bacall—Betty—lunched with him. Betty could
always be depended upon to arrive at Romanoffs in a smash-
ing Paris outfit. Led by the maitre d' or by Mike himself,
Bogie and Betty would step royally through the archway and
down three steps into the main dining room. With a room-
ful of eyes riveted upon them, it played just the way Mike
had planned it. The Bogarts rarely dined alone. No sooner
did they order than one of their crowd might appear and at
Bogie's invitation be invited to sit down. On a given day,
these might include any of the following: screenwriter
Nunnally Johnson, Holmby Hills neighbors Judy Garland
and her husband Sid Luft, Bogie's agent, Irving (Swifty)
Lazar, writer Nathaniel Benchley, composer Jimmy Van
Heusen, Frank Sinatra, or Mike Romanoff himself.

The game—Bogie's game—was to arrange the crowd in such a way that one of his guests would be compelled to pay the bill. It was a cruel game in a way, with Swifty Lazar most often the unwitting victim who picked up the tab. One could avoid being victimized by simply not accepting Bogie's invitation. But who in the world would have declined such an offer—not one celebrity in all of Hollywood!

Only the proprietor was immune to Bogie's game; not even Bogie would dare push the bill on him. He had once tried to enter Romanoffs without a tie and was turned away. In that instance, however, he returned with shoes unlaced and the laces tied around his neck. Mike looked him up and down, both front and back. Bogie was admitted.

When Bogie was not working, he was inclined to sit alone at Romanoffs well into the afternoon. Mike invariably would join him after the crowd thinned. If Bogie seemed down in spirit, Mike might call up one of his standby tales about the vagaries of married life. Like most Romanoff stories, it would begin in quite a different realm:

My friend, I see you are eating that damned French toast and sausage again today. . . . Believe it or not, I once knew a sausage maker. We made a spring Atlantic crossing together some years ago. . . . Oh, that was a beautiful time in my life. Cudahy was the fellow's name, quite a talker, and he stuck to me like a chameleon the whole voyage. I think he was afraid someone might kidnap him and hide him in the dog kennel. There weren't a lot of places to stash a body on that ship; the kennel would not have been a bad choice. . . .

Can you imagine anyone, though, kidnapping a sausage maker? But that is indeed what happened to Cudahy not long before we met. Some damn fools in New York had taken him hostage. They demanded a substantial ransom, and his family came up with the payment! Cudahy never let on what they paid to set him free—but I would wager that ten pounds of the stuff you're eating right now might have done the trick. That

Best of friends Mike Romanoff and Humphrey Bogart
Courtesy Globe Photos Inc.

sausage is absolutely the most expensive on the market these days. . . .

I sometimes wonder how large a ransom might be demanded for a kidnapped restaurateur—not much, I bet. I can picture it now, the kidnappers insisting that Gloria pay dearly for the return of her sequestered husband. Gloria's a shrewd one, Bogie, and I can see her now: "Six tins of Romanov caviar and one case of Dom Perignon—not a whit more!"

If such as this failed to revive Bogie's spirits and send him on his way, then Mike would bring out the chessboard. For

155

the next hour the prince would match wits with the king. Sometimes the game went on for days, but the prince always won. If there ever was a man in Beverly Hills with whom Michael Romanoff could form a lasting friendship, it was Humphrey Bogart. Sadly, the friendship would be cut short.

Sometime in 1955, Bogie was dallying with his "lunch bunch" in a smaller party room upstairs. Betty walked in, looked around, and observed: "I see the rat pack is all here." That's how it all began. In mock seriousness, they decided to form an organization. First of all, they appointed officers: Frank Sinatra, pack master; Judy Garland, first vice president; Sid Luft, cage master; Swifty Lazar, recording secretary; Nathaniel Benchley, historian; Lauren Bacall, den mother; and Bogie, public relations. Jimmy Van Heusen, Mike Romanoff, David Niven, and Noel Coward were members without portfolio.

"[The Rat Pack] exists for the relief of boredom and the perpetuation of independence. We admire ourselves and don't care for anyone else." So proclaimed Humphrey Bogart to the press.[51]

That was only part of the story. There was a whole set of loose rules to be followed: Be "at home" to another rat whenever there was a light on in the house, stay up very late and drink a great deal, never "rat on a rat," don't take anything seriously, and always be frank with each other, which meant being as rude as one could be. Betty Bacall put it in other words:

> We had principles. You had to stay up late and get drunk, and all our members were against the P.T.A. We had dignity. And woe betide anyone who attacked one of our members. We got them.[52]

And that's how it often turned out. Judy Garland and Sid Luft lived next door to the Bogarts. If any rat came to call at Bogarts, the Lufts were there too. Judy drank much too much and fought constantly with Sid. Bogie thought Sid had no class at all and frequently reminded him of the fact. No one liked Judy's drinking, yet no one dared throw her out. With the Lufts, it was always just one miserable evening. Frank Sinatra was the charmer in the crowd. He and Bogie were supposed to be the best of friends. Everyone found Frank fascinating, especially Betty. Bogie was less than pleased, for he knew too much about his friend's sexual escapades. For sure, the Rat Pack was not strong on mutual trust. It could count on raunchy rudeness and clever put-downs whenever a few rats gathered. Apparently that was enough. The pack's strength really derived from Humphrey Bogart's popularity and the very human tendency toward exclusivity. What then was the role of Prince Michael Romanoff?

One can hardly imagine Mike Romanoff hurling insults at a fellow rat across the room or laughing uproariously at another rat's predicament. His wasn't that kind of humor, and he rarely drank to excess. Intellectually he was far above all the others, with the possible exception of Bogart. One can only guess that Mike Romanoff—little Harry Gerguson—found in the Rat Pack the "persons whose lives I believe to be adorned." For Mike, that was enough.

Humphrey Bogart first became ill in 1956, soon after the Rat Pack came into being. It was a battle against cancer that began in the throat and then spread through his entire body. As Bogie's health deteriorated, his Rat Pack—for indeed he was at its center—became his support group. Twice during the illness Bogart had surgery. Twice each day Romanoffs delivered to the hospital foods that Mike thought would please, if not cure, his friend. When Bogie was at home, Mike would call in the afternoon, stopping by between Romanoffs lunch and dinner hours. Betty was invariably at the studio, for during the time of Bogart's illness, she made several films.

Alone with Mike, Bogie would attempt the irreverent banter for which he was so well known. But it had become increasingly painful for him to talk. Better to turn the conversation over to his friend.

"Old man, remind me again about that Frenchman who fell on his face." Mike would look upward, wrinkle his brow, and close his eyes, feigning the deep concentration necessary to draw out this much-faded memory.

Ah, my friend, that was a time when you and I were much younger, not long after the Great War. I recall that Paris had come alive with victory, but she was still a bit tattered; I might add that so were we all. I was courting a young Habsburg princess at the time—God, what a beauty she was. And we had much in common, for we were both refugees from fallen empires and desperately poor as well. Somehow I had gotten together a few francs so that we could spend an evening at the Moulin Rouge—a first time for both of us. I had even bought a corsage for the princess and she wore it with such pleasure.

We took a table discreetly removed from the stage, for the front tables were left to the cruder men. Young and old and without inhibition, these men lusted after the girls of the Moulin Rouge. I ordered two glasses and a bottle of decent wine; then we sat back to enjoy the evening—the princess and I.

The music began, and the dancers emerged from either side of the house. Oh, what a sight they were, prancing across the stage, kicking up their legs, bouncing their boobs and wiggling their rear ends so coyly. . . . I must admit, Bogie, the costumes left much to be desired. Like most of Paris, the Moulin Rouge had not yet shaken off the wartime economies and it really showed—especially the garlands of wilted silk flowers that covered the dancers' posteriors.

Between acts we were entertained with the naughtiest of French boulevard songs and, when the dancers returned, by the gentlemen in the front seats who hung shamelessly over the stage to see what there was to see.

Holmby Hills Rat Pack in 1956, left to right: Humphrey Bogart, Sid Luft,
Lauren Bacall, Judy Garland, Ellie Graham, Jack Entratter,
Mike Romanoff (partly hidden), Frank Sinatra, Gloria Romanoff,
David Niven, Hjordes Niven.
Courtesy Bison Archives/Marc Wanamaker, Los Angeles

*As it turned out, during the finale there was much to see.
The dancers were into the final cancan, the entire line racing
toward the rear, when one of the garlands fell to the stage,
revealing a pair of the damndest little cheeks. Yet bare naked
as the unlucky dancer was, she kept up admirably. The entire
line continued toward the back of the stage, seemingly oblivi-
ous of her calamity.*

*Slowly from the front row rose a stone-faced gentleman—we
gasped, for we recognized him as a well-known member of the
government, minister without portfolio no less. Holding him-*

159

self erect with some difficulty, he ascended to the stage, picked up the garland, and proceeded in slow motion toward the retreating dance line. Presumably his intent was to return the garland to its proper rear location, but at that moment the dancers swung around to begin the march forward. From our table we could see a disaster in the making; yes, the surprised young lady of the missing garland slammed right into the French minister without portfolio, and he promptly fell to the stage.

Ah, so well trained were those girls. They just stepped right over the prostrate minister and made their final dash to the footlights, never missing a single beat. The curtain came down behind them and the place went wild. Bogie, you had to see it to believe it. Everyone was throwing flowers to the stage. ' *And even my lovely princess tore the corsage from her shirtwaist and prevailed on me to cast it forward with the others.*

We drifted apart after that night, the princess and I. Yet I feel eternally bound to this Habsburg beauty for our having shared one magical evening at the Moulin Rouge.

Bogie would never be satisfied with such an ending to this infamous Romanoff tale. "Come on, Mike, tell it straight— about that Frenchman." And so, only reluctantly, Mike would supply the missing punch line.

"You are right, my friend. Three days later it all came out in the press: The unfortunate minister without portfolio was dead, having been struck down by a fatal stroke days earlier at the Moulin Rouge, where he was discussing affairs of state backstage with the director." Bogie would smile and perhaps be warmed by his friend's reluctance to speak of death.

"Better to die at home, eh Mike?"

Time for the queen to return from the studio and Mike to be on his way.

Humphrey Bogart died at home on January 15, 1957. He was just fifty-seven years old. Word reached Romanoffs immediately. Mike and Gloria were the first to arrive, followed by all the others in the Rat Pack except Sinatra, who was in New York. It was a church funeral followed by crema- tion, with Mike Romanoff as one of the pallbearers. Afterward everyone went back to the Bogarts' home. Romanoffs had sent over casseroles, salads, cheeses, and liquor, along with a captain and two waiters, all three dressed in their distinctive red jackets. This would be Prince Michael's last act of fidelity to the one man in Hollywood he could truly call a friend.

The story of Romanoffs waiters: It is a tale by itself. Where once they had dressed in crisp white jackets, now they were a symphony of royal crimson. And where once the staff of waiters comprised a mix of Central European immigrants, now at Romanoffs II, it was strictly Italian. Only the Teutonic maitre d' survived from the old order, and in this time he was Kurt Niklas. Though this proud German never admitted to it, his primary character trait—the driving force in his life—mirrored that of his employer. No one must know his roots!

Kurt was a child of the Nazi system—his "Aryan" mother unmarried and his Jewish father a traveling salesman who had a wife and children elsewhere. Kurt's father was beaten to death by the Gestapo, for consorting with an Aryan. Kurt was denied an education, then an occupation, finally his freedom. He escaped with his life, for in physiognomy he matched his mother—tall and blond with pale blue Nordic eyes. He also learned to survive by his wits. When Kurt turned up in Los Angeles, he vowed never to reveal his past, at least not his Jewish forebears. First as a waiter, then as cap- tain, and finally as Romanoffs' last maitre d', Kurt Niklas was a caricature of the German elite—suave, precise, and impossibly arrogant. For all the public knew, he might once have been an SS officer. Rather let them believe that than reveal the truth. So insecure was the man who brought Prince Michael through the final restaurant years.

At Romanoffs in Beverly Hills, Mike needed all the help he could get. He had established Romanoffs on Nob Hill in San Francisco, and more recently, Romanoffs on the Rocks out in Palm Springs. Neither prospered. Only too late did Mike learn that the success of Romanoffs lay in the magical illusion it created. Where but in Hollywood could such a fragile illusion prevail? And even in Hollywood it wouldn't last forever.

In March 1958, the United States Congress passed a bill declaring Michael Romanoff to be a legal resident of the United States, having entered the country on December 22, 1932. The bill had first been submitted in the House by Beverly Hills Representative Donald Jackson, who also introduced letters of recommendation, including one from J. Edgar Hoover, director of the FBI. In the House Judiciary Committee, it was recorded that "the Justice Department has been unable to prove that Mr. Romanoff was born outside of the United States and he has been unable to prove birth in this country," noting Mr. Romanoff's claim to have been born in New York on February 21, 1893. The committee noted further that Romanoff married an American citizen on July 4, 1948, that his annual income was $20,000 (the equivalent of $200,000 in 1996) and his assets $350,000—he was a very prosperous man.

President Dwight D. Eisenhower signed the bill into law on May 16. Across the land it became national news with front-page coverage—from New York, to St. Paul and Minneapolis, to Hillsboro, Illinois, and on to Los Angeles and elsewhere. The following day, *New York Times* columnist Inez Robb wrote with great affection:

> Before it is forever too late, this peasant today rushes into print with a petition to Prince Mike Romanoff to cease and desist from his present efforts to go legit. . . . .
>
> That Mike, nature's self-made nobleman, should crave the benediction of the law in his sunset years is a lamentable

Customs Officer Helene Lawrence congratulating
New Citizen Mike Romanoff at the L. A. Federal Building
while Gloria looks on, June 27, 1958
Courtesy *Herald Examiner* Collection/Los Angeles Public Library

triumph of conformity over rugged individualism. In his old
free-wheeling, free-loading days, Mike was not so much without the law as above it. For him now to ask shelter within its
arms is no less shattering to his loyal subjects than the abdi-
cation of Edward VIII. . . .

He lived on the richest cuffs in the country, and many of
us envied him his imperial brass. It seems so sad now, as time
is taking its toll of the Russian Romanoffs, that respectability
is taking its toll of the American branch. . . .

Probably where Mike went wrong—that is, got off the
royal road—was at the point where he finally latched onto
some money of his own. When he left New York, started that
Hollywood restaurant, and met with explosive success as a
restaurateur, conservatism set in. Money of one's own is
always a sobering experience. That's what did it, if you ask
me. . . .

163

The law is for those of us who plod in conformity from the cradle to the casket. It is not for Ariel, nee Romanoff.

I would remind the Prince there is such a thing as noblesse oblige before he puts himself irretrievably on the side of the law.

O, say it ain't so, Mike! Say it ain't so.*

Miss Robb's plea notwithstanding, Mike immediately applied for U.S. citizenship. On June 27, he appeared before Los Angeles Federal Judge Ernest A. Tolin, who took him aside and asked, "Mr. Romanoff, as you are probably aware, nobody who has a title can become a citizen without publicly renouncing that title."

Mike snapped his arm skyward and declared in a firm base voice, "I hereby renounce any title to the claim that I am prince of all the Russians."

This satisfied the judge. Mike was sworn in together with a hundred others. Afterward he was quoted as saying,

The importance of the sense of belonging doesn't occur to somebody who already belongs. There is a great deal of spiritual quality about it. You probably can't understand it if you've never known anything but being a citizen.

To simply not exist, legally, is not a pleasant thing. This sense of belonging is a very important element. It is like a person who has always been well—he cannot appreciate how a sick person feels. It is a spiritual sickness not to belong.[54]

It was to be the greatest Fourth of July ever—Mike Romanoff's party to celebrate his new citizenship. Gloria too had a place in the celebration, for it was their tenth wedding anniversary. Mike started out by announcing his intention to invite a thousand of his best friends. As it turned out, just six hundred were invited, to dinner at 7 P.M., and they were virtually all celebrities. The newspaper

---

*This expression goes back to the 1919 Black Socks baseball scandal and a small boy confronting Shoeless Joe Jackson: "O, say it ain't so, Joe. . .

The grand Fourth of July party at Romanoffs, left to right:
Citizen Mike Romanoff, Mrs. Robert Rowan, Mervyn Leroy,
Laraine Day, Leigh Battson
Courtesy *Los Angeles Times* Photographic Archive/University
of California, Los Angeles

published a few of the names—Winthrop Rockefeller, Zsa
Zsa Gabor, Henry Ford, Alfred Vanderbilt, Leo Durocher,
and Congressman Donald Jackson. One can imagine that
film celebrities were out in full force, including all the old
Rat Pack, along with the new, for since Frank Sinatra had
taken over from Bogart, it was quite a different crowd.

Not invited were hundreds of loyal Romanoffs patrons,
film society, and others who had always considered themselves the best of friends with the prince. Mike's July 4 bash
turned out to be a watershed in the rise and fall of
Romanoffs. The restaurant business depended on the mul-
titudes who dined there year in and year out, in some cases

day in and day out. They came at first to see celebrities, but that gets old very soon. Their loyalty was sustained by good food, immaculate service, and most of all, a curious feeling of kinship with the man who ruled it all. Thus the great Fourth of July celebration, meant to acknowledge the pinnacle of Mike's aspirations, rather presaged his restaurant's downfall. Business at Chasen's in Hollywood picked up significantly while Romanoff''s suffered empty tables. Mike understood why, but it was too late.

17

Old Man of the Rat Pack

I am closing at the end of this month. It's the end of an era. There is no longer room for a restaurant of this kind. Its operation is much too costly. . . . There is a new type of snobbery—a shirtless, coatless, tieless type of snobbery. They don't want to go anywhere where they have to dress. . . .

At first I was depressed, but now I'm beginning to look forward to a new life. I feel a sense of adventure. I'd become much too complacent. Now I feel an exhilaration I haven't felt for many, many years.[55]

Frank Sinatra's Rat Pack had little in common with the Rat Pack that had once congregated at homes in Holmby Hills. Frank was in charge—charming, unpredictable, and irascible. Long gone was Lauren Bacall, whom he had so energetically courted before and after Bogie's death. Frank had assembled a distinctly different Rat Pack—Dean Martin, Sammy Davis, Peter Lawford, Joey Bishop, Shirley MacLaine, Tony Curtis, Sammy Cahn, and Harry Kurnitz. Two of the originals were still there—Swifty Lazar and Jimmy Van Heusen—but they were hardly visible. Oddly enough, the name of Prince Michael Romanoff was grouped in a special category known as "Rat Pack Affiliates," along with Peter Lawford's brother-in-law, Senator—later President—John F. Kennedy.[56]

Walter Winchell with Gloria and Mike, 1958
Courtesy Bison Archives/Marc Wanamaker, Los Angeles

The new Rat Pack rarely stayed home. They still gathered at Romanoffs, often in the penthouse, but they traveled unceasingly—to Lake Tahoe or Las Vegas for all-night gambling, especially when one of them was performing on stage, to Palm Springs, to London, to Paris or the Riviera—wherever Frank Sinatra had a hankering to visit.

Romanoffs was still booking the best of the private parties—Grace Kelly's farewell bash, Academy Award parties before and after the Oscar* presentations, New Year's Eve extravaganzas, and celebrations of various kinds by old friends like Spencer Tracy, David Niven, and Darryl Zanuck.

*Oscar® is a registered trademark of the Academy of Motion Picture Arts and Sciences.

Presiding over yet another Romanoffs event: Prince Michael
and friends, 1959
Courtesy Bison Archives/Marc Wanamaker, Los Angeles

And the tourists still came, for an exquisite lunch and in
hopes of catching a glimpse of the stars. Travelers from
Hillsboro invariably booked luncheon at Romanoffs, just to
bask in the glory of a hometown boy who had made good.
On one such occasion, the family asked the waiter to inform
Mr. Romanoff that they'd like to bring him greetings from
Hillsboro. The waiter returned with the curt message that
Mr. Romanoff had never heard of Hillsboro. Yet later, as the
family left the restaurant, there was Mike at the door: "Give
my regards to Clint Bliss."

When a young couple named Weyerhaeuser booked a
reservation for dinner, Mike Romanoff took note. During
dinner he stopped to greet them at their table: "I once knew
the St. Paul Weyerhaeusers. Such fine people they were."

But the tourist trade couldn't do it alone, and the film celebrities who once vied for the preferred restaurant tables were increasingly conspicuous by their absence. If the tourists didn't notice, for sure the proprietor did. Over too many years had these celebrity connections been the bolster, hence the energizer, for Mike's fragile ego and creative genius. Once during the fading restaurant years a local film producer was entertaining a pair of shipping tycoons at lunch. It was a business meeting of the highest stakes. Yet the proprietor repeatedly passed by the table, directing a beseeching nod to the host. When the host finally understood Mike's ploy, he called him over and introduced him to the president of the Orient Shipping Lines and the president of Cunard Lines. Obviously satisfied, Mike promptly diasppeared into the kitchen.

Mike's absences from Romanoffs likewise became more frequent and longer in duration. Too often he was trailing along with the Rat Pack to Palm Springs and New York, to London and Paris, even to Moscow and Leningrad. Without his presence, the Hollywood trade simply went elsewhere.

For Citizen Mike, the places abroad were especially delicious, for they represented the magical life he had designed for himself in his youth—the boulevards, the hotels, the cafes and other haunts of an imagined aristocracy. Where once he had been the consummate outsider, now he traveled in the company of Sinatra, the king. What sweet vindication of an entire life journey!

Visiting Russia was something else. This was the era of the Cold War, and for sure Vilna was out of bounds, but that hardly mattered. Mike barely remembered his childhood, and in any case, all traces of the Geguzins and their community had vanished under the Nazis. Yet he twice visited Russia in these years, once as part of Frank Sinatra's entourage and once in the company of William Keck, Jr., heir to the Superior Oil Company fortune. Never mind that

Mike's brother Yuri lived and prospered in Moscow as director of theater repertoire for all of the Soviet Union. Mike never made contact, for that would surely have ended Yuri's career if not his freedom. In Leningrad lived sister Fanya, she who had survived the German siege during the Second World War—900 days—while her husband, daughter, and son all starved to death, along with a million other Leningrad citizens. Neither did Mike make contact with Fanya for fear of doing her harm. It was enough just to know she too was there in St. Petersburg, the city of his most vivid fantasies.

Back home in Beverly Hills there was a bit of very good news. 20th Century-Fox Studios was preparing to make a film about his extraordinary life journey; for starters they gave him $75,000 just for the privilege. A screenplay had already been completed by Luther Davis, author of at least four successful film scripts.* The title of the film was to be *Instant Prince.* The project gave evidence of a crowning glory, indeed a vindication, of Mike's entire life. Unfortunately, for reasons unknown, the film was never made.

Then another wonderful opportunity presented itself. Frank Sinatra was to give a concert in Haifa, Israel, a benefit concert for a children's home in Nazareth. He invited Mike to come along on his private plane.

Haifa—Mike learned that his niece Nina, from Vilna, had just settled there. Years earlier he had vowed to seek out this daughter of his sister Ida Marshak, who was sacrificed to the Holocaust. But as long as Nina lived in Soviet-controlled Lithuania, it was virtually impossible. Nina Papermacher, her husband Joseph, and daughter Dahlia stayed in Lithuania for a decade after the war, until Joseph was attacked on the street for daring to be a Jew. The

---

The Hucksters, The Gift of Love, Holiday for Lovers, and *Kismet.*

171

Papermachers were able to leave Lithuania, settle briefly in Poland, and finally obtain an exit visa to Israel.

To their absolute amazement, one afternoon a limousine stopped at their modest apartment building. Out of the vehicle stepped the famous American film star Frank Sinatra, and with him was none other than the fabled Uncle Hersh. The only problem was that although both Nina and Joseph could speak Lithuanian, Russian, Polish, Yiddish, and Hebrew, they and Nina's uncle had no language in common. An English-speaking neighbor was sent for—by that time the whole neighborhood was gathered around the limousine—and for an hour, two branches of the Vilna Geguzins were reunited. When it was time to leave, Frank Sinatra pulled from his pocket two tickets to his concert. With a grand gesture, he handed them over to the Papermachers. As if to upstage his more famous companion, Mike began pulling a mass of U.S. paper currency from his various pockets, until they were empty and turned inside out. All of it he gave to Nina, and then he kissed her hand. Later the Papermachers counted the bills—$1,200— enough to build a home of their own.

The upstaging of Frank Sinatra in Haifa was not limited to Nina Papermacher's modest apartment. The following day at the benefit concert, Frank was paired on stage with Israel's most beloved folk singer of the time—Ester Ofarin. Quite likely it was because of Ester that the house sold out so early. As reported by the press later, in loving detail, the adored Ester was magnificent. And by the way, the American singer Frank Sinatra also performed. Not surprisingly, Sinatra was less than pleased; he couldn't get out of the place soon enough.

The tale of the Haifa concert became a staple in Mike's library of anecdotes. It was always related with some discretion, though, for Mike still knew his role when it came to Frank Sinatra and the Rat Pack.

Mike Romanoff in Russia, ca. 1960
Courtesy Bison Archives/Marc Wanamaker, Los Angeles

1962, the last year of Romanoffs: It began in a typical Rat Pack way. Frank Sinatra and Dean Martin were invited to play cameo parts in a film starring Bob Hope, Bing Crosby, Peter Sellers, and Dorothy Lamour. The film was *The Road to Hong Kong,* the last of a long list of "road" films by Hope and Crosby. The cameo was scheduled to be filmed in London. Frank invited Mike to come along, and the three of them flew off to London. It was a curious trio, two young men who always seemed to have mischief on their minds, accompanied by a gentleman a generation older. It may be that Frank invited Mike along as an act of filial loyalty to the man who had become his father figure. Or it may be that together Dean and Frank invited him along to have a convenient victim for their practical jokes. Given the turn of events after the brief filming, the latter seems the more probable.

After the filming, the three men went out on the avenue, Mike in an elegant London outfit that included bowler hat and umbrella. They stopped at a shop where one could select fabric, then have a tie made up. Mike ordered six ties, to be delivered to his hotel room. Then he went back to the hotel for a nap. Dean and Frank went to work; they intercepted the ties; cut the threads on each one where the two strips connected behind the neck; and carefully repackaged the ties. When Mike awoke and joined his companions for a drink, Frank presented him with the boxed ties.

"Thank you, my friend, I give you the Volga River," said Mike. (He had the custom of presenting grand gifts to close friends who did him favors—the Volga River, the Ural Mountains, St. Petersburg, and the like.) Mike opened the first box, took the tie out, and placed it around his neck— where it fell in two long strips. He opened the second box, the third, and so on. In each case, the tie fell apart. He was furious. The next day the three men returned to the tie shop. Mike nearly threw the ties into the clerk's face, even as the clerk was insisting that the ties had left the shop in good order. At that moment, Frank and Dean began to laugh. It had all been a practical joke, fomented by Vic Damone, a mutual friend who also happened to be in London.[57]

Such good friends they all were!

Frank had brought along to London a carton of Chesterfield cigarettes, Mike's favorite brand. Beforehand he had "fixed" each cigarette package—opening the cellophane and the package from the bottom, pulling out the cigarettes, cutting them in half, returning them to the package, then repairing the package and the cellophane. It was a slow and exacting task. Frank had phoned ahead to the Savoy Hotel in London to have "fixed" cigarette packages placed in Mike's room. In London, he even had "fixed" packages delivered to the restaurant where the trio intended to have dinner.

For Mike, too, it started out as a joke, but he became increasingly exasperated as it played over and over again. It was not until after the trip, and the long flight home to Los Angeles, that it finally became too much for Mike. He arrived home absolutely exhausted, but Gloria insisted on inviting Frank and Dean in for a drink. Mike picked up a fresh package of cigarettes from the coffee table, opened it, and once again pulled out stubs. So Gloria was in on it also! Mike lost his temper. He ordered his two friends out of the house and fell into his bed.[58]

Such fun they all had when the Rat Pack came together!

That summer the final tragedy of Marilyn Monroe was played out. Marilyn had been involved with the president of the United States. When the time came that he didn't want to be involved with her any longer, he sent his brother, the U.S. Attorney General, to break the news to Marilyn. How Bobbie Kennedy broke the news to her is not clear. There are many versions of this tale. What is clear is that Marilyn Monroe transferred her obsession with Jack Kennedy to his brother Bobby. She pestered him in many ways, including numerous phone calls to his Washington office and also threats of exposure, relayed through the Kennedy brother-in-law, Peter Lawford. Everyone in the Rat Pack knew of the problem, and Marilyn only made it worse by her increasing dependence on sedative drugs and alcohol.

It is far beyond the scope of this tale to speculate on events in the last year of Marilyn Monroe's life. What is of interest here, however, is the deep and abiding friendship between Gloria Romanoff and Marilyn, a friendship that apparently had its beginnings back in 1948 when Marilyn first became noticed in Hollywood. Possibly they met at Romanoffs, for Marilyn was a luncheon regular. In those days, this was the place and noon was the time for an aspiring actress to meet the casting directors and other Hollywood prospectors.

Gloria was to witness the evolution of a beautiful young woman, who did indeed reach the top in stardom, only to be destroyed later through drugs, alcohol, and misuse by others. After Marilyn's death, Gloria was inclined to comment on several occasions:

> My view would not be a popular one. This was a girl who, early on, probably did whatever was necessary to get rolling in the business. As time passed, Marilyn, I think, became somewhat indifferent to sex. She didn't have any overwhelming need to be with men, and I think it had a lot to do with those early years.[59]

The affection between these two women—Gloria and Marilyn—would be lifelong, especially in the late years when both were connected to the Rat Pack one way or another. During the summer of 1961, Marilyn was for a time Frank Sinatra's "woman," and it seems wherever Marilyn turned up that summer, there were the Romanoffs also. Gloria remembered the Sinatra summer as a flawed time in Marilyn's life: "There were several incidents when she had been mixing drink and sleeping pills, and had to be revived—very close calls."[60]

In August Marilyn spent a weekend on Frank's yacht and shared his cabin. Once again, Gloria and Mike were there. Afterward Gloria commented on what a pitiful weekend it had been.

> [Marilyn] was taking sleeping pills, so she'd disappear at ten o'clock at night and not be awake till eleven or twelve the next day. We kidded Frank, saying, "Some romance this is!"[61]

It was the following January that the first open meeting between Marilyn Monroe and Robert Kennedy took place. Peter Lawford and his wife, Pat Kennedy Lawford, were entertaining Bobby and his wife, Ethel, for dinner. Other guests included Kim Novak, Gloria and Mike Romanoff, and Marilyn, who became Bobby's designated dinner partner. Gloria described the evening as one in which Marilyn was being very political, speaking in opposition to the United States policy in Vietnam. Bobby was at first impressed, then displayed amusement when he noted that she kept referring to scribbled notes on a card stashed away in her purse. After dinner, "Kennedy called his father long-distance to say he was seated with Marilyn Monroe, and would his father like to say hello to her!" Indeed Marilyn did greet the elder Kennedy over the phone. Such were Gloria's recollections of that curious evening.[62]

Marilyn's obsession with the attorney general seems to have had its origins that night. From then on, both her physical condition and her state of mind were of constant concern to friends. Frank Sinatra was a partner in the Cal-Neva Lodge, a gambling casino at Lake Tahoe. His friends were often there on weekends, especially when Frank was performing. Peter Lawford was a regular at Cal-Neva Lodge, with or without his wife. Marilyn, too, was often in tow, along with Gloria and Mike. Presumably the Romanoff presence would distract Marilyn from what seemed to be a case of chronic despair. These were invariably Rat Pack kinds of weekends—fun and alcohol. On the second weekend in July, at least for Marilyn, it became a great deal of alcohol and very little fun. Marilyn would surely have died that weekend but for the intervention of Peter Lawford. Tipped off by the casino switchboard, to which Marilyn kept an open line, Peter and Pat (Kennedy) Lawford rushed to Marilyn's room and found her drugged and barely conscious on the floor. In Gloria's version of that night:

Marilyn drank champagne, and some vodka, then took sleeping pills. The Lawfords walked her about, after midnight, trying to keep her awake, and I think they called Frank in, too. I remember Marilyn telling me one of her problems was that she'd taken pills so long, they didn't work for her the way they did for other people. So she'd begin about nine in the evening and build up that lethal combination of booze and pills.[63]

For Marilyn Monroe, it all came to a tragic end the first weekend in August. It was the same scenario as at Lake Tahoe when it came to drugs and alcohol—a desperate call and an open line—but this time Bobby Kennedy's reputation was at stake. (Earlier in the day he may have visited Marilyn, no doubt intent on persuading her finally to leave him and his brother alone.)[64] Saturday evening at about 7:30 P.M., Marilyn called Peter Lawford. Her voice was groggy: "Say good-bye to Jack, say good-bye to Pat, and say good-bye to yourself, because you're a nice guy."[65]

She must have dropped the phone after that, for Peter called her back several times, but the line was always busy. He now guessed that she was possibly unconscious; but rather than be seen going to her home, he called his manager, who presumably would intervene in a more discreet manner, and then a friend who lived near Marilyn, all this to protect his brothers-in-law, the president and the attorney general. There are several versions as to what happened after that, but clearly by midnight Peter Lawford was very drunk and Marilyn Monroe was dead.

Romanoffs also was in its final throes. Two distinct events would seal its fate. One evening in fall, Herbert Marshall had a reservation for 7:00 P.M. at his regular table No. 1 (at noon, after Humphrey Bogart's death, No. 1 was always reserved for Spencer Tracy). Shortly before 7:00, Marshall phoned to say that he and his party would be late—9:00 P.M.

at the earliest. Just then, Abe Lastvogel of the William Morris Agency walked in with a party. Noting Marshall's later reservation, the maitre d' asked Lastvogel if he would like table No. 1. Of course; no one would turn down table No. 1. All went well until 9:00, when Herbert Marshall walked in. The Lastvogel party was still drinking its final coffee. The assistant maitre d' invited Marshall and his party to have drinks at the bar until Abe Lastvogel and his friends were finished. The actor was incensed and demanded to speak to Mike Romanoff.

"Hey Mike, how come you've given away my table when I was good enough to phone and say I'd be late?" Mike simply exploded.

"Who ever said that table belongs to you. This is my restaurant, and why don't you pompous British asses get the hell out of here." Marshall promptly left with his party, never to return. Mike went into the kitchen, sat down, drank two double martinis, one after the other, put his head in his hands, and cried.

Not long after this episode, one of the waiters made a serious error. A well-known Hollywood personality ordered vichyssoise with curry. When it arrived at the table, there was no curry in it. She protested; the waiter argued. Mike Romanoff heard the rumpus and promptly fired the waiter. As it turned out, Mike's was the more serious error.

The fired waiter was the union steward. The following day a union representative called on Mike and demanded that he rehire the man and, further, that Mike call a meeting of all the employees and apologize to the waiter in front of the entire group. Mike was forced to oblige.

Afterward he asked Kurt, his maitre d', how many bookings they had for December—a goodly number, as it turned out.

"Good, we'll close at the end of the year."

The closing of Romanoffs was almost as sad as the fact that Romanoffs closed.

Bart Lytton, an old friend of Romanoffs, invited Mike to his home to discuss plans for a final New Year's Eve party. Mike brought along Kurt Niklas, who by now was not only maitre d' but also the catering director. Lytton presented his plan: Since Romanoffs could seat six hundred people comfortably, on three floors, he would invite three hundred guests and Mike should invite three hundred guests. Lytton would pay for it all. It seemed to be a most generous gesture by an old friend. Mike agreed to it, and he began to make plans with Kurt.

As the time drew near and the guest lists took shape, enter Frank Sinatra. This was no way to close down Romanoffs. All Lytton wanted was for his friends to meet Mike's more famous Rat Pack friends. Mike should invite a hundred friends to the penthouse for their own private party, while Lytton and his friends could carouse below on the first two floors—no mixing, urged Frank. In these years, Frank Sinatra had a great deal of influence over Mike, perhaps more influence than any single person had ever had on him. Mike finally agreed and then went about informing Lytton. Lytton was furious, even threatened a lawsuit, for the time was so short. It was a bad ending all around.

On New Year's Eve, Bart Lytton hosted a party of four hundred at his home. It was catered by Dave Chasen of Chasen's restaurant in Hollywood. Over at Romanoffs, Billy Wilder hosted a party of 114 in the penthouse—the Rat Pack and friends. The rest of Romanoffs' cavernous spaces were dark. Such was the final farewell.

18

End of the Reign

It is impossible to understand the appeal of this charmer—
and he had enormous charm—if you start to analyze him as
a merely successful imposter. He was in his own person a
marvelously sustained gag. He did not pretend to be Prince
Michael Romanoff of Russia. He pretended, and managed,
to be a great comic pretending to be Prince Michael
Romanoff of Russia. . . .

Most Americans, I believe, think of title as decorative and
also comic. All hail, then, a man who by caricature exposed
the pretensions of nobility in countries which have long
been republics. Mike Romanoff was a one-man satire on the
whole French and Italian jet set. He simply decided to be a
prince and chuckled up his enormous cuffs to see the
descendants of genuine noble houses kow-tow and haggle
for a choice reservation in his restaurant.—*Alistair Cooke,
1979*[66]

The decade of the sixties was indeed the end of the reign.
President John F. Kennedy was assassinated in November
1963. He was succeeded by Lyndon Johnson, a president
who had no ambitions at all when it came to Hollywood and
film stars. Then in June of 1968, Robert Kennedy was assassinated in a Los Angeles hotel. It all marked the end of
Camelot as well as a deepening of the war in Vietnam, a new
time in America, a time of change for Mike Romanoff.

In 1964 he sold his restaurant property for a tidy sum. The
developer demolished the building and built a modern lux-

ury office complex where Romanoffs once stood. Mike lent his Romanoff-Oxford accent, along with his imperial bearing, to several Hollywood films: *Goodbye Charlie* with Tony Curtis, Debbie Reynolds, Pat Boone, and Walter Matthau; *Do Not Disturb* with Doris Day; *Caprice* with Doris Day and Richard Harris; *Von Ryan's Express* and *Tony Rome* with Frank Sinatra. It was on the set of *Von Ryan's Express* that nineteen-year-old actress Mia Farrow first succumbed to the Sinatra charm. Oddly enough, Mike Romanoff had also been present eight years earlier at the first encounter between Mia and Frank. Director John Farrow was having dinner at Romanoffs with daughter Mia. Sinatra passed by the table and took one look at her. "Pretty girl," he commented to Farrow. "You stay away from her," retorted the father.[67] And so had Sinatra done until after Farrow's death early in 1963.

Whatever Sinatra's failings might have been in these years, he was clearly devoted to his old friend, the prince. After Frank and Mia were married, they saw a good deal of Mike, dining with him regularly. And when Mia dared ask the old man if he really was a prince, "he just twinkled until I did too."

Mike traveled to Miami with Frank to film *Tony Rome,* and he undertook a nationwide tour with Doris Day to promote *Do Not Disturb.* But it was strenuous, keeping up with the youngsters, as Mike was wont to complain.

Mike's last maitre d', Kurt Niklas, opened his own restaurant on North Cañon Drive. He named it The Bistro and patterned it after Romanoffs. Mike's old patrons came by in droves. At first it was difficult for him to see his maitre d' succeeding in a business where he believed he had ultimately failed. Almost thirteen years they had worked together—Mr. Romanoff and Kurt. Neither knew much of the other's family life, but they did share knowledge of each other's intimacies. Along the way there had been romantic dalliances in both their lives. Each knew something of the other in this regard; neither had ever spoken of it, anywhere. It was a curious sort of male bonding.

Gloria and Mike Romanoff were frequent patrons of The Bistro. Kurt always gave them a preferred table and always addressed them as Mr. and Mrs. Romanoff. He still knew his place. It was during a lunch at The Bistro that Mike signed a contract with Harper and Row Publishers. He would finally write his memoirs. Over the next several years, Mike did indeed complete the task, but he simply couldn't bear to release the manuscript.[68]

In the summer of 1971, Gloria and Mike sold their home on North Beverly Drive. Mike stopped by The Bistro and reported the news to Kurt. The Romanoffs planned to travel around the world and then settle in New York. But first Mike intended to put on one more grand party, inviting eighty friends for dinner to celebrate his eightieth birthday. Would The Bistro furnish the wine—a white Chateau Latour along with a red wine? Kurt cautioned his old employer, who by now had almost become a friend. Certainly he had both wines in stock, but Chateau Latour was the most expensive French wine on the market.

"I know it's expensive, Kurt, but at my age you want me to be cheap?"

Kurt smiled. It struck him that Mike was pale, and looking very old. Grasping for words of friendship, he volunteered, "Look, Mr. Romanoff, this eightieth may be *your* party, but *I* intend to put on the eighty-first."

Mike shook his head. "You're too late, Kurt; it's already past." And so it was. Mike Romanoff had turned eighty-one on February 21 of that year.

The following Friday, Mike Romanoff had lunch at the Beverly Hills Hotel with Bob Evans, who at that time was one of Hollywood's major movie moguls. Producer David Brown of 20th Century Fox stopped by their table to chat. He was a long-time friend of Mike's and in fact had for years owned the film rights to Alva Johnston's *New Yorker* series profiling the earlier life of the prince.

Mike shared with this friend the plans he and Gloria were making now that the house was sold. After the eightieth birthday bash, they would leave immediately for Europe via New York. Mike promised to phone Brown from New York, for he too was soon to leave for Europe. They would arrange to meet somewhere on the continent. But it never came to pass.[69]

After lunch, Mike stopped at a Beverly Hills bookstore, intending to load up on his favorite recreational reading— European history, both fiction and nonfiction. It was in the bookstore that he was stricken with a heart attack. Taken by ambulance to Good Samaritan Hospital, he died a few days later. It is said that on his deathbed, Mike asked Gloria to burn his memoir manuscript. Presumably she obliged, for to this day it has never surfaced.

That evening Gloria Romanoff was quoted in the *Los Angeles Times:*

> [Mike] didn't like funerals, said they were a crashing bore. He did say a couple of times that if some of his friends ever wanted to have a memorial service, this was okay—providing it be short, held late in the day, and within reasonable proximity to a decent bar.[70]

The death of Mike Romanoff, like so much of his life, was national news. Across the land newspapers published obituaries, photos, brief biographies, and eulogies, retelling for the third and fourth time tales of his extraordinary adventures.

Nunnally Johnson, Hollywood film director and good friend to Mike over many years, summarized it rather well:

> A real prince is an accident. Mike made it by his own efforts. It only goes to show what a good American boy can do if only he applies himself.[71]

* * *

A quarter century after the prince's death, a few of those who remember are still with us.

Elizabeth Nissen, who first met Harry in his early Paris days, is alive and well in Minneapolis. An avid reader of *The New Yorker* and *The New York Times,* she has followed his adventures over an entire lifetime, discovering little to alter her initial dismay.

Alistair Cooke, whose observations still earn him the affection of Americans everywhere, continues to find the "Imperial Mike" a character worth knowing. Paul Mellon, that great and gentle philanthropist, still remembers Mike from his student days—"never intoxicated, amusing and interesting, a very likeable chap."

Robert Bliss of Hillsboro, Illinois, who back in 1936 slipped Mike a five-dollar bill "for a spot of petrol," has been publisher of the *Montgomery County News* for many years now. Recently, in his weekly column, he retold the tale of Harry Ferguson who became Prince Michael Romanoff, Hillsboro's most famous citizen.

Kurt Niklas, Romanoffs last maitre d', is currently writing his own memoirs—the dozen years at Romanoffs and more than thirty years with his own Bistro restaurants. He acknowledges that although Mike Romanoff's Hollywood fame derived from that of his more famous friends, in truth it was his own distinct persona that attracted: "Romanoff was so ugly he was beautiful and as raconteur he had no equal."

Oleg Cassini holds equally respectful memories of the prince—"a superb actor, who played a preposterous role, yet carried it through consistently and with elegance."

Mia Farrow, hardly more than a child when Romanoffs restaurant closed, speaks of this old family friend with great affection—"I don't remember Michael ever saying very much, but he radiated such sweetness. . . . He was a lovely man."

Mike Romanoff's own family is amazingly intact.

Olga's son Emmanuel Piore is long retired from an illustrious scientific career, crowned with numerous honors and an honorary doctorate. He and his wife, Nora, winter on Manhattan and summer at Martha's Vineyard. Dr. Piore remembers his Uncle Hersh as "a man of affairs, who was always kind to my mother and me." Mrs. Piore says of Gloria Romanoff, "She was the most beautiful and accomplished person one could imagine."

Ida's daughter Nina Papermacher and her husband still live in Haifa, Israel, near where Uncle Hersh and Frank Sinatra once visited them. Their daughter Dahlia married an American, Richard Friedman. By coincidence he is grand-nephew of the Austrian-born artist Lionel Reiss, whose painting of the Vilna ghetto Prince Michael once admired on a Paris street.* The Friedmans live in Belle Harbor, New York. Nina frequently comes from Israel to visit daughter Dahlia's family and the Piores. Says Nina of her Uncle Hersh, "He was a very generous man."

Gloria Romanoff lives in southern California. She has declined to be interviewed.

*See page 13 for "Vilna Ghetto" and page 20 for "Orchard Street in New York," both painted by Lionel Reiss.

Remarks on One Man's Life

Jonathan Jensen, M.D.

I never knew Michael Romanoff the man, not to mention Hershel Geguzin the child. However, in my medical practice and in my academic career, I have indeed come across his kind, both the man and the child. In commenting on such a life, one must acknowledge first that analysis based solely on historical material leaves open many questions. Accepting this caveat, 1 nevertheless put forth some observations with reasonable conviction.

In the normal development of a child, the task of separating from the parent at age two or three requires, first, a parent who nurtures and provides consistency. A second component is that the parent allow the child to express him- or herself in gradually developing independence. By age three, the child is then able to part from the parent and take along an internal representation of that supporting person. The healthy three-year-old typically knows that the parent will come back, even when they are separated.

The behavior and character traits of Michael Romanoff have their origins in his earliest childhood. The child Hershel was denied a normal development. At the time Hershel was born, his mother was most likely in mourning. Her husband had been killed, and her energies were of necessity focused on survival, supporting the six children and herself. Consequently, she was unable to give sufficient attention to her youngest child. This deficient relationship between mother and son played out very early in the son's misbehavior during his earliest years in Vilna. His truancies from school, defiance of authority, and running away from home are all evidence of poor boundaries and his desire for attention.

When at the age of ten Hershel was sent to the new world, he did indeed experience actual abandonment. Even then, it was not his mother but rather his older sister Olga who saw him off on the train with his relatives. Having never developed a satisfactory attachment to his mother, Hershel was ill-equipped to deal with the pain of separating from her.

His imitation of others and his taking on the accouterments of various lifestyles should be viewed in light of the severe circumstances that prevented his mother from giving him sufficient nurturing. A child who develops an imitative style of life typically has a passive, distant, or absent father. The child's mother, on the other hand, tends to be demanding, controlling, and generally unable to provide the emotional support required for the child to develop his or her own identity. Such a child, like Hershel, continually fears abandonment. In Hershel's case, this emotional poverty was probably to blame for his not developing a conscience. The development of a mature conscience requires that the child of five, six, or seven gradually give up his or her own impulses and desires so as to earn the respect and affection of a trusted, respected adult. Hershel's early history in Vilna reflects his inability to respond to parent or school authorities appropriately. In New York City, his failure to attach to the Bloombergs, his incorrigibility in the Manhattan Hebrew Orphanage, and his placement in the Juvenile Asylum all confirm this inability to respond to internal cues. He was forced to behave according to the external limits set on him.

"Harry" continued his string of broken relationships, with one benefactor after another being disappointed in any attempt to form a relationship with the boy. He controlled his fear of rejection by acting so outrageously that each time he was forced to leave. As he grew to young adulthood, he became increasingly able to assimilate the trappings of his surroundings. This ability to lose himself in the role of people he had come to admire goes far beyond the usual actor's "willful suspension of belief." In fact, for Harry it was a state indistinguishable from reality; he was unable, despite his considerable intelligence, to separate out emotionally what his desires were, where his impulses led him, and what the real world of limits, budget concerns, and possibilities offered.

Harry's assumption of the persona of a member of the Russian royal family is in fact typical of a fantasy that is experienced by many six- and seven-year-old children. Dubbed the "family romance," this fantasy has many children believing that the parents who are so unable to allow them to express their every wish and gratify their every impulse cannot possibly be their real parents. Their real parents, of course, must be kings and queens who have unlimited income and unlimited power and would allow the child's every id wish. Thus, the adult Mike Romanoff's identification with the Russian royal family allows him to live out these early fantasies and grant all of his early imaginings. Unable to integrate the good or the bad in other people or in himself, he acts as if all of his fantasies are true.

The fact that others not only somehow understood that Mike Romanoff's imaginings derived from these early strivings but were often enchanted by them points to the remnants of such fantastic wishes in all of us. Whereas most of us have been able to dream our dreams and contain these urgings, expressing them in hobbies or turning them into creativity through art and literature, Romanoff turned them into action. Mature defenses such as altruism, sublimation, and suppression were unavailable to him. Only later in life was he able to stumble upon the successful formula of participating in the play life of adults. Among the movie stars, those symbols of fantasy, Romanoff was on common ground. In Hollywood, he was able to use his intelligence and his imitative skills to weave his caricatures into a unique social network.

In the end, Mike Romanoff's story is one of sadness, of multiple losses, of repeated attempts to form long-term, consistent attachments replaced by the transient enjoyment of fantastic pursuits. His highly colorful successes speak to his extraordinary intelligence, his repeated downfalls to his inability to negotiate the limitations of reality. Mike Romanoff did indeed lack the mature coping mechanisms that carry ordinary men and women through satisfactory lives. Yet, a quarter century after his death he is still remembered vividly by those whose acquaintance with him was casual at best. I find this remarkable.

JONATHAN JENSEN, M.D.
ASSOCIATE PROFESSOR OF PSYCHIATRY, UNIVERSITY OF MINNESOTA,
DIPLOMATE OF THE AMERICAN BOARD OF PSYCHIATRY AND NEUROLOGY
IN GENERAL AND CHILD PSYCHIATRY

Citations

1. Joe Stephens, *Springfield State Register*, 1987.
2. *Montgomery County News*, March 20, 1923.
3. Ibid.
4. *St. Louis Star*, March 17, 1923.
5. *Montgomery County News*, March 20, 1923.
6. *The New York Times*, November 29, 1922.
7. *St. Louis Star*, March 15, 1923.
8. *The New Yorker*, October 29, 1932, p. 22.
9. *Hillsboro Journal*, March 20, 1923.
10. *St. Louis Star*, March 15, 1923.
11. *St. Louis Star*, March 17, 1923.
12. *The New Yorker*, November 12, 1932, pp. 24–5.
13. Dahlia Friedman, New York, May 21, 1995.
14. *The New Yorker*, November 12, 1932, p. 25.
15. *Los Angeles Examiner*, August 27, 1927.
16. *The New Yorker*, November 12, 1932, p. 26.
17. *Los Angeles Examiner*, August 27, 1927.
18. *Los Angeles Times*, October 1, 1927.
19. *Los Angeles Times*, April 15, 1931.
20. *The New York Times*, May 9, 1932.
21. *New York Herald Tribune*, January 8, 1933.
22. *The New York Times*, December 24, 1932.
23. *The New York Times*, December 29, 1932.
24. Alistair Cooke, *The Americans*, p. 61. This excerpt is presented with the permission of Alistair Cooke.
25. *The New York Times*, January 18, 1933.
26. *The New York Times*, April 4, 1935.
27. Alva Johnston, "The Downfall of Prince Mike," *The Saturday Evening Post*, March 20, 1943.
28. *Montgomery County News*, October 22, 1936.
29. Ibid.

30. Ibid.
31. *Los Angeles Herald,* April 24, 1937.
32. Irving Lazar, *Swifty: My Life and Good Times,* pp. 37–8.
33. *Time,* June 19, 1939, p. 33.
34. Lucius Beebe, "Prince Mike's Place," *Holiday,* March 1954.
35. Ibid, p. 67.
36. Hume Cronyn, *A Terrible Liar: A Memoir,* pp. 160–1. This excerpt is presented with the permission of Hume Cronyn.
37. Ronald Headland, *Messages of Murder: A Study of the Reports of the Einsatzgruppen of the Security Police and the Security Service, 1941–1943,* pp. 74, 123.
38. *Los Angeles Herald Examiner,* July 5, 1948.
39. Hedda Hopper, *From Under My Hat,* pp. 296–7.
40. *Life,* October 29, 1945, pp. 141–4.
41. Gene Sherman, *Los Angeles Times,* September 15, 1946.
42. Kurt Niklas, Beverly Hills, October 26, 1995.
43. *Time,* February 23, 1948, pp. 8–9.
44. *Los Angeles Times,* July 5, 1948.
45. Lucius Beebe, *Holiday,* March 1954, p. 67.
46. *Los Angeles Times,* January 21, 1951.
47. Lucius Beebe, "Prince Mike's Place," *Holiday,* March 1954.
48. David Brown, *Let Me Entertain You,* p. 118. This quote from J. Edgar Hoover is presented with the permission of David Brown.
49. Ibid.
50. Joe Hyams, *Bogie: The Biography of Humphrey Bogart,* p. 132.
51. Kitty Kelley, *His Way: The Unauthorized Biography of Frank Sinatra,* p. 239.
52. From an interview with Paul O'Neill of *Life* magazine, as quoted in Richard Gehman, *Sinatra and His Rat Pack,* pp. 49–50.
53. *The New York Times,* March 17, 1958.
54. *Los Angeles Herald Examiner,* June 28, 1958.
55. *Los Angeles Herald Examiner,* December 12, 1962.
56. Richard Gehman, *Sinatra and His Rat Pack,* pp. 52–3.
57. Nancy Sinatra, *Frank Sinatra, My Father,* pp. 157–59.
58. Ibid.
59. Anthony Summers, *Goddess: The Secret Lives of Marilyn Monroe,* pp. 37–8.
60. Ibid, p. 241.
61. Ibid, p. 232.
62. Ibid, pp. 245, 247.
63. Ibid, p. 284. Also, James Spada, *Peter Lawford, The Man Who Kept the Secrets,* p. 314.
64. Ibid, p. 318.
65. Patricia Seaton Lawford, *The Lawford Story,* p. 163.

66. Alistair Cooke, *The Americans,* p. 64. This excerpt is presented with the permission of Alistair Cooke.
67. Mia Farrow, *What Falls Away,* p. 86. This excerpt is presented with the permission of Mia Farrow.
68. David Niven, Jr., whose late secretary typed the complete memoirs, November 1994.
69. David Brown, *Let Me Entertain You,* p. 116.
70. *Los Angeles Times,* September 2, 1971.
71. Alistair Cooke, *The Americans,* p. 65.

Bibliography

Unpublished Sources

Oral History

Bliss, Robert, telephone conversation, June 21, 1995.

Brady, Jack, personal communication, Capitola, California, April 25, 1997.

Cassini, Oleg, telephone conversation, December 28, 1995.

Friedman, Dahlia nee Papermacher, telephone conversation, November 19, 1994; personal communication, New York, May 21, 1995.

Mellon, Paul, telephone conversation, September 8, 1995.

Niklas, Kurt, personal communication, Beverly Hills, June 27 and 28, 1994, October 26, 1995; telephone conversation, May 10, May 19, and December 2, 1995.

Nissen, Dr. Elizabeth, personal communication, Minneapolis, December 22, 1992, August 25, 1993, and February 5, 1994.

Papermacher, Nina nee Marshak, personal communication, New York, May 21, 1995.

Piore, Dr. Emmanuel and Nora nee Kahn, personal communication, New York, November 18, 1994.

Sivertsen, Sarah Maud nee Weyerhaeuser, telephone conversation, September 16, 1995.

Weyerhaeuser, Nancy (Mrs. F. T.), telephone conversation, August 8, 1995.

Written Correspondence

Farrow, Mia, dated March 24, 1997.

Gleason, Joseph T., archivist, The New York Society for the Prevention of Cruelty to Children, New York, with enclosures, dated July 5, 1995.

BIBLIOGRAPHY

Harvard University Archives, Cambridge, Massachusetts, dated June 20, 1994.

Howard, Robert G., Clerk of Court, Family Court of the State of New York, New York, dated July 5, 1995.

Kanter, Hal, Encino, California, dated April 11, 1994.

Nissen, Dr. Elizabeth, Minneapolis, Minnesota, dated November 6 and 20, 1994, and October 17, 1995.

Niven, David, Jr., Los Angeles, California, dated November 16, 1994.

Papermacher, Nina nee Marshak, Haifa, Israel, translation from the Polish by Dahlia Friedman, dated April 21, 1995.

Penn, Gelah, Communications Associate, Jewish Child Care Association of New York, New York, with enclosures, dated June 26, 1995.

The Children's Village, Dobbs Ferry, New York, with enclosures, dated June 28, 1995.

Published Sources

Libraries where major Published Sources were accessed

Hillsboro Public Library, Hillsboro, Illinois

Litchfield Public Library, Litchfield, Illinois

Los Angeles Public Library, Los Angeles, California

Minneapolis Public Library, Minneapolis, Minnesota

St. Louis Public Library, St. Louis, Missouri

University of California, Los Angeles, California: University Research Library

University of Illinois, Urbana–Champaign, Illinois: American Library Association Archives

University of Minnesota, Minneapolis, Minnesota: The Wilson Library

Newspapers

Hillsboro Journal, Hillsboro, Illinois

Illinois State Register and the *State Journal Register,* Springfield, Illinois

Litchfield Daily Herald and *Litchfield News-Herald,* Litchfield, Illinois

Los Angeles Examiner and *Los Angeles Herald-Examiner,* Los Angeles, California

Los Angeles Times, Los Angeles, California

The Minneapolis Journal, Minneapolis, Minnesota

Minneapolis Tribune, Minneapolis, Minnesota

Montgomery County News, Hillsboro, Illinois

New York Herald-Tribune, New York, New York

St. Louis Star, St. Louis, Missouri

St. Paul Dispatch, St. Paul, Minnesota

The New York Times, New York, New York

BIBLIOGRAPHY

Other Periodicals

Holiday, 1952
Life, 1945
The New Yorker, 1932
Newsweek, 1947, 1948, and 1958
The Saturday Evening Post, 1943
Time, 1939, 1948, and 1952

Book Sources

In Search of Identity

Beider, Alexander, *A Dictionary of Jewish Surnames from the Russian Empire.* Teaneck, New Jersey: Avotaynu, Inc., 1993.

Fry, Annette R., *The Orphan Trains.* New York: New Discovery Books, 1994.

Glazer, Nathan, and Moynihan, Daniel Patrick, *Beyond the Melting Pot: The Negroes, Puerto Ricans, Jews, Italians and Irish of New York City.* Cambridge, Massachusetts: The M.I.T. Press and Harvard University Press, 1963.

Holt, Marilyn Irvin, *The Orphan Trains: Placing Out in America.* Lincoln, Nebraska: University of Nebraska Press, 1992.

Miller, William H., Jr., *The Great Luxury Liners: 1927–1954.* New York: Dover Publications, Inc., 1981.

Seeger, Charles Louis, *The American Library in Paris.* New York: Trustees of the American Library in Paris, 1925.

Thompson, Susan Otis, "The American Library in Paris," *The Library Quarterly,* American Library Association, Chicago, Illinois, April 1964.

On the Fringe of Society

Cooke, Alistair, *The Americans.* New York: Alfred A. Knopf, Inc., 1979.

Hauberg, John H., Jr., and Sweeney, Catherine Hauberg, *Weyerhaeuser and Denkmann.* Rock Island, Illinois: Augustana Book Concern, 1957.

Irwin, Will, *Highlights of Manhattan.* New York: The Century Co., 1927.

Massie, Robert K., *The Romanovs: The Final Chapter.* New York: Random House, 1995.

Mellon, Paul, with Baskett, John, *Reflections in a Silver Spoon: A Memoir.* New York: William Morrow and Company, Inc., 1992.

At Home in the Land of Illusion

Arad, Yitzhak, *Ghetto in Flames, the Struggle and Destruction of the Jews in Vilno in the Holocaust.* Jerusalem, Israel: Yad Vashem, 1980.

Brown, David, *Let Me Entertain You.* New York: William Morrow and Company, Inc., 1990.

BIBLIOGRAPHY

Cronyn, Hume, *A Terrible Liar: A Memoir.* New York: William Morrow and Company, Inc., 1991.

Gentry, Curt, *J. Edgar Hoover: The Man and the Secrets.* New York and London: W. W. Norton & Company, 1991.

Goodman, Ezra, *The Fifty-Year Decline and Fall of Hollywood.* New York: Simon and Schuster, 1961.

Headland, Ronald, *Messages of Murder: A Study of the Reports of the Einsatzgruppen of the Security Police and the Security Service, 1941–1943.* London and Toronto: Farleigh Dickinson University Press, 1992.

Hopper, Hedda, *From Under My Hat.* Garden City, New York: Doubleday & Company, Inc., 1952.

Lazar, Irving, with Annette Tapert, *Swifty: My Life and Good Times.* New York: Simon & Schuster, 1995.

Levin, Dov, *Fighting Back, Lithuanian Jewry's Armed Resistance to the Nazis, 1941–1945,* translated from the Hebrew by Moshe Kohn and Dina Cohen. New York and London: Holmes & Muir, 1985.

Nelson, Nancy, *Evenings with Cary Grant: Recollections in his own words and by those who knew him best.* New York: William Morrow and Company, Inc., 1991.

Powers, Richard Gid, *Secrecy and Power: The Life of J. Edgar Hoover.* New York: Macmillan, Inc., 1987.

Toledano, Ralph de, *J. Edgar Hoover: The Man in His Time.* New Rochelle, New York: Arlington House, 1973.

With Friends Who Mattered

Bacall, Lauren, *By Myself.* New York: Alfred A. Knopf, Inc., 1978.

Cooke, Alistair, *The Americans.* New York: Alfred A. Knopf, Inc., 1979.

Farrow, Mia. *What Falls Away.* New York: Nan A. Talese/Doubleday, 1997.

Finch, Christopher, *Rainbow: The Stormy Life of Judy Garland.* New York: Grosset & Dunlap, 1975.

Frank, Alan, *Humphrey Bogart.* New York: Exeter Books, 1982.

Gehman, Richard, *Sinatra and His Rat Pack.* New York: Belmont Books, 1961.

Hyams, Joe, *Bogie: The Biography of Humphrey Bogart.* New York: The New American Library, 1966.

Kelley, Kitty, *His Way: The Unauthorized Biography of Frank Sinatra.* New York: Bantam Books, 1986.

Lawford, Patricia Seaton, with Ted Schwarz, *The Peter Lawford Story.* New York: Carroll & Graf Publishers, Inc., 1988.

Shipman, David, *Judy Garland: The Secret Life of an American Legend.* New York: Hyperion, 1992.

Sinatra, Nancy, *Frank Sinatra My Father.* Garden City, New York: Doubleday & Company, Inc., 1985.

BIBLIOGRAPHY

Spada, James, *Peter Lawford: The Man Who Kept the Secrets*. New York: Bantam Books, 1991.

Spoto, Donald, *Marilyn Monroe: The Biography*. New York: HarperCollins Publishers, Inc., 1993.

Summers, Anthony, *Goddess: The Secret Lives of Marilyn Monroe*. New York: Macmillan Publishing Company, 1985.

Index and Guide to Names

Major sources include *Encyclopaedia Britannica, Who's Who in America, Who's Who in Hollywood,* and *Who Was Who on Screen*

213

Other Books by Jane Pejsa

Available through Kenwood Publishing

- *The Molineux Affair* — Soft cover, 240 pages — $12.95

- *Matriarch of Conspiracy: Ruth von Kleist 1867–1945* — Hard cover, 400 pages — $24.95
  Soft cover, 400 pages — $19.95
  German-language hard cover — $32.00

- *To Pomerania in Search of Dietrich Bonhoeffer: A Traveler's Companion and Guide,* Second Expanded Edition — Soft cover, 70 pages — $7.50

- *Gratia Countryman: Her Life, Her Loves and Her Library* — Soft cover, 340 pages — $14.95

All books may be ordered through your bookstore or directly from Kenwood Publishing, 2120 Kenwood Parkway, Minneapolis, MN 55405-2326. Minnesota residents add 6.5% sales tax. Add $3.00 shipping for a single book; add $1.00 for each subsequent book in the order. Your personal check payable to Kenwood Publishing is welcome. By E-mail: Pejsa@sprintmail.com. We accept the following credit cards: American Express, Discover/Novus, Mastercard, VISA. Specify credit card number and expiration date.